HARVESTING EXCELLENCE
BY ALAIN DUCASSE

© 2000 Assouline Publishing
Photographs © 2000 Axel Icard
Cover illustration © Michel Sinier and
Assouline Publishing

Quotation from *Skinny Legs And All*
by Tom Robbins
© 1990 Bantam

Assouline Publishing
601 West 26th Street
18th floor
New York, NY 10001
USA

www.assouline.com

ISBN: 2 84323 191 4

Printed in France

HARVESTING EXCELLENCE
BY ALAIN DUCASSE

ASSOULINE

To Gwénaïlle
and all the food artisans whose dedicated
work allows our profession to exist

ALAIN DUCASSE

JOURNALISTS

Jean-Christian Agid
with
Patricia Gaviria

PHOTOGRAPHER

Axel Icard

TABLE OF CONTENTS

The American food revolution

Farmers, ranchers, and fishermen have launched a food revolution in the United States. Within the past twenty years they have used natural soils and waters, pastures and grains to reach incomparable flavors in food. The results are on the table with baskets of crisp, porous bread, spoons of molten cheese, slices of tender, rare meat, and vegetables that snap under the fork. What Americans have done, is harvest excellence.

The incredible bounty found in the United States invites us, the chefs, and those who cook in their own kitchens to elicit the finest subtleties in food. I have always been enticed by the challenge to blend my French *savoir-faire* with the profusion of American flavor. Since a superior plate is one that respects the natural qualities of food, I constantly strive to release the elements of each ingredient while effecting a certain harmony. With the enormous range of products in this country, the creative potential is boundless.

Since the age of twelve, when I told my grandmother that she overcooked her green beans, I have been consumed by a curiosity for food. Despite my wonderful experiences in France, I still have an insatiable desire to seek greater knowledge, pleasure, and surprise in cooking. The United States has opened doors of inspiration to me, which, much like the kitchen doors of my grandparents' farm in southwest France, I look forward to walking through.

To begin, I am what you may call a beef-aholic. After cooking for more than twenty-five years, I truly believed that I had tasted all of the best beef—from the Japanese Kobe and Argentinean steak, to the French Charolais. I have recently discovered, however, a red meat from the Arizona mountains that inspires absolute, childlike delight. This tenderloin is sublime. From the first bite, the meat melts tender yet robust in the mouth. Upon sampling it, I sensed a distinct character and history to the meat. I tasted the wide grasslands, touched with a hint of the wild, in which the cattle had roamed. What created such subtly and texture? I had to find out and share my discovery.

A food experience reaches unparalleled heights when the consumer knows the source of the product, specifically, the people who take the time and care to nurture their harvests. After all, while the *je ne sais quoi* of a chef begins with the proper ingredients, the ingredients come only from the *savoir-faire* of the harvesters.

When I was devising recipes for *The Washington Post* some fifteen years ago, my friend Jean-Louis Palladin, whom I'd known since my early years in Michel Guérard's kitchen in Eugénie-les-Bains, provided me with ingredients. When he moved to Washington, D.C., in 1980 as chef of *Jean-Louis* at the Watergate Hotel, Palladin imported most of his food products from France. Frustrated with the slow, painstaking process, he traveled across the United States in search of new and innovative producers. Visiting farms, ranches, and orchards, Palladin told the producers exactly what he, as a chef, was looking for. A trusting relationship evolved between Palladin and producers and as finer products made their way to his kitchen, finer cuisine was served at his tables.

Fellow chefs also conducted searches for the best food products in America. David Bouley, Daniel Boulud, Terence Brennan, David Burke, Tom Colicchio, Gilbert le Coze, Christian Delouvrier, Rocco Di Spirito, Jean Joho, Thomas Keller, Laurent Manrique, Michael Mina, Charlie Palmer, Jean-Francois Payard, Sylvain Portay, Michel Richard, Eric Ripert, Michael Romano, Marcus Samuelsson, Günter Seeger, Julian Serrano, Joaquim Splichal, Laurent Tourandelle, Charlie Trotter, and Jean-Georges Vongerichten—they all established their own personal

relationships with harvesters. Sirio Maccioni, the head of *Le Cirque 2000* in New York, also contributed greatly to the development of upscale cuisine. The resulting alliances have elevated the quality of food to today's remarkable heights.

While each region has drawn from its *terroir* -- the climate, soil, and sun -- to yield singular products, the flare and individuality of the multiple cultural influences in the United States have set the stage for modern American cuisine.

Beyond the beef from Arizona, there are cheeses, from New York to California, that rival French ones. Fish from Maine stands as some of the best in the world, and the warm Florida seas yield an unique class of fish with outstandingly fresh flavors. In the Midwest, farmers tend their gardens with palpable patience, allowing vegetables to grow slowly and simply, cultivating succulent tenderness. And in Ohio, there is an exquisite peach, a fruit that I want to look at closely, touch, caress, and smell before even picking it from the tree.

The list could go on indefinitely, and this book is by no means exhaustive. Knowing the energy, care, and devotion that American producers put into their products, and then having tasted the results, I would like to pay tribute to them all.

This book opens like a menu—with bread, the most basic, fundamental, and spiritual of foods. It closes with a philosophy—with love, patience, and knowledge, anyone can harvest excellence. In between is a journey in taste. And whether you read the following stories all at once or a bit at a time, I hope that you will regard food and cuisine with a new and enlightened perspective, as I have upon visiting the United States. Your joy in cooking and dining may be enhanced, because you will know the story.

Alain Ducasse
New York, June 19, 2000

BREAD

Bread that sings

The sun has just risen over the North Pacific coast, painting the December horizon with a variety of pinks and grays. Overhead, however, the sky is still a midnight blue as Chad Robertson walks across his backyard in Point Reyes, California. As he does every morning, Robertson is going to his bakery just steps away from his house which, even at this hour, is warm with the rustic aroma of fresh baking.

A few hours later, he fills the shelves of the Bay Village Bakery with large loaves of fresh bread. Still snapping and smoking from the heat of the deep wood-fired oven, they seem to sing as steam slowly whistles out. Glowing beneath the amber-colored crusts, the loaves are ready to be savored by a small number of lucky people who know good bread.

Nothing in life destined Robertson to move to California and bake bread. Born in Texas in the early 1970s, he knew as a child only that he wanted to work with his hands. His appreciation of craft-work was inherited from his artisan grandparents who are among the last people in the United States to make hand-tailored cowboy boots. Though content in his grandparents' workshop, Robertson found himself gradually drawn to the world of food and travel. At age eighteen, he left Texas and moved east to study at the Culinary Institute of America in Hyde Park, New York.

"I was not interested in baking initially," Robertson remembers. That was, until he and his future wife, Elisabeth Prueitt, visited a bakery in the Berkshire Mountains in western Massachusetts. An unexpected passion blossomed on the spot. Robertson inquired with Richard Bourdon, a baker he knew in Housatonic, Massachusetts, if he could be his apprentice. The baker agreed, but stipulated that the position would not be paid. To help the young couple, however, Bourdon offered them free housing as part of the arrangement. Salary was unimportant to Robertson and he jumped at the opportunity. "As soon as we finished school in 1992, we left for Housatonic, and I worked for Bourdon for a year and a half."

In the green misty hills of the Berkshires, Robertson had found his calling. "I was working, without pay, fourteen-hour days that started at three o'clock in the morning. But I didn't think anything of that. I was smitten with the craft."

At the same time, Elisabeth began to devote her life to her own passion: *pâtisserie*. She became a pastry chef at a spa in Massachusetts and supported the couple through Robertson's apprenticeship. When Bourdon's head baker left, Robertson filled the job and received his first wages as a professional baker.

Despite their early success, Robertson and Elisabeth wanted to move along and learn more secrets of

the singing bread. "It was important to seek out people who taught us traditional methods," Elisabeth reminisces. With this in mind, they spoke continually of their dream to visit the country known for the best bread in the world, France.

Bourdon nurtured this ambition. "He was always talking about his mentor, a French baker from the Alps named Patrick LePort, with whom he had worked twenty years before," Robertson tells with a fond smile. "I was so young and impressionable, to hear Bourdon's story of a wood-fired oven in the French mountains was thrilling," he admits almost sheepishly. "It was sticking in my head."

Bourdon called LePort to discuss a possible apprenticeship for the young American baker and before they knew it, Chad and Elisabeth were on a plane bound for Savoy.

Life in France was not so different from life in the Berkshires. The couple stayed in a room just above the bakery and, when not hiking the snowcapped Alps, they patiently learned traditional French baking methods.

"What I learned in France was how to use the wood-fired oven," Robertson says of his early time in Europe. "I also wanted to learn the French style of *levain*, or leavening, and the virtues of enhancing the bread's flavor with fresh mountain water." In technical terms, levain is the yeast that makes the bread rise and which gives it an earthy flavor. The French levain resembles dough and is made of a mixture of flour and high-quality spring water that is left to ferment naturally through the growth of inherent wild yeast and bacteria. Because it consists of natural agents, the levain can take up to two to three days to rise. In order to achieve the desired texture and enhanced wheat flavor, however, the wait is necessary.

"In America, we use a dough that has more of a sour aspect, while in France there is a lot of energy spent on producing a dough that doesn't keep too much of this flavor," Robertson explains. According to him, the bitter element kills some of the wheat and fermentation flavors. "The bread just gets acidic," he observes and adds, "the French flour is also much lower in gluten, so the French bread, to me, has a crisper crust and much more tender interior. And it keeps better."

At LePort's suggestion, Chad and Elisabeth moved to the south of France to complete a second apprenticeship with baker Daniel Collin. Living in a small cottage among vineyards, the two rode their bicycles every day to the bakery. Under the tutelage of Collin, Robertson used a wood-fired oven to make traditional country bread. "It was a very romantic period," muses Robertson. Massachusetts was far behind them, Texas even further.

After three months in the Var region of southern France, Robertson felt the time had come to head home and open his own bakery. His mission now was to reproduce in the United States the same flavorful wood-fired bread he had baked in France.

The challenges of moving to the United States became evident immediately. Not only did Robertson need to find a wood-fired oven and an ideal setting in which to bake, but he had to have access to the right blend of flours. "We came straight to Marshall, California, north of Point Reyes, because Alan Scott, the only man in the United States we knew of who built wood-fired ovens, lived there," Robertson explains.

Upon arriving, they both fell in love with northern California. "We were looking for a region with an abundance of food and wine that resembles the French countryside, and we wanted to be close to the ocean as well as a city," Robertson says. The wild coast north of San Francisco offered a divine bounty of food: oysters, abalone, salmon, milk, cheese, fruit, lamb, duck, herbs, and an infinite variety of wine from the Sonoma and Napa valleys. Equally important, "we wanted to be close to the people actually producing the food."

The young couple soon befriended the nearby craftsmen——mainly farmers, builders and woodworkers. Within little time, they found a plot of land, zoned for both business and residential use, just feet away from the Tomales Bay Food Market in Point Reyes.

Having found a wood-fired oven and a desirable settling place, Robertson's dream-bakery was beginning to come to life. Finding the right flour, however, proved more difficult.

"I have been trying every kind of flour I can find, and blending different qualities to try to achieve the textures that I loved when I was in France——that is, a more tender crumb that stays moist longer, keeps better, and is easier to digest." He holds a thick slice, squeezing the crust between his fingers, "I also learned in France the importance of stone-ground flour." Robertson firmly believes that the finest white flours are those that have been stone-milled and sifted. Through this process, the oils from the germ are rubbed into the flour, releasing much more of the wheat flavor and adding "a more supple texture." However, flour with a higher oil content does not store well beyond six months to a year, "in the States now, most flour is roller-milled, and the oils are, therefore, taken out immediately so that the flour can keep much longer." Today, Robertson uses products that are grown in Utah, Idaho, and North Dakota, stone-milled locally in San Francisco, and delivered, fresh, to him once a week.

He deliberately wants to keep his bakery a one-man business, allowing only his wife to help when needed. "It is hand-making the bread from the very beginning to the very end," explains Elisabeth. "It is one person's expression."

Robertson takes particular care with each loaf. He regularly checks the cooking status of his oven fueled by walnut and almond wood. When a loaf is ready, he carefully pulls it from the oven, lets it cool for a few seconds, and then brushes off the ashes by hand before resting it on a shelf. A warm scent of nut and grain invades the space, testing one's restraint not to tear into a loaf with bare hands. In less than an hour, the loaf will be sold next door at the Tomales Bay Food Market along with some complementing cheese or ham.

Without any fellow workers, Robertson has deviated from the normal schedule of a baker. "I decided that I didn't want to be working all night," he says categorically. Since the production remains small -- no more than 200 to 250 loaves a day -- Robertson has only two or three hours of baking. After he delivers his country loaves, his baguettes, his walnut, sesame, corn, and olive breads, he eats a light lunch and catches a nap before he heads back to the bakery. In the afternoon, he mixes and shapes his dough before letting it cool for twelve hours at a constant temperature of 50°. "It allows me to have the rest of the afternoon and the evening off."

As he kneads his dough, Elisabeth practices her art at her traditional patisserie not far away in Mill Valley. Naturally, she puts her husband's bread up front on the shelves.

"It is hard work, but it is an art and a craft that we enjoy," says Chad.

Robertson acknowledges his good fortune in finding this spirit of place in Point Reyes and laughs merrily, if not in disbelief, at the exchange value of his bread there. He points to a peel -- a long wooden pole with a flat board at the end -- which bakers use to place loaves into, and remove from, the oven. It is slim and delicately designed of cypress and walnut wood. "A neighbor gave it to us for trading bread," smiles Robertson. Indeed, the baker exchanges his bread for a variety of foods, including oysters, fish, mushrooms, wine and cheese. "It is not always an even trade, but our neighbors are very generous: three breads for a goose, one for a wild salmon, three or four for a bottle of wine or some abalone. At certain times of the year, my gain can be quite abundant."

And when Chad the baker and his wife, Elisabeth, need more money they simply bake more bread, creating a choir of the singing loaves.

"The bread baked with levain keeps well - it has both a taste and a smell. I like it thickly sliced and toasted on one side only, with salted butter."

ALAIN DUCASSE

CHEESE

The artisan cheese maker

Jonathan White learned to cook the old-fashioned way, "with my eyes, nose, and mouth," he declares. Taught as a young boy by his grandmother, who did not read or write, he grew up understanding the need to watch ingredients in action. "When an illiterate person teaches you how to cook, you don't learn how to measure temperature and volume." Today, White closely watches milk as it heats, curdles, and ripens into some of the finest butter and artisanal cheeses in Upstate New York.

A former engineer, White first experimented with making cheese in his kitchen in Hoboken, New Jersey. The result was far from gourmet, and White blamed both the recipe he followed and the packaged milk he used. Discouraged, he returned to designing robotic joints and made goat cheese, albeit without high-quality milk, only as a hobby.

But the pastime became consuming and ten years later White began to consider becoming a professional *fromager*. Leaving urban life, he moved to the New York countryside with his wife and child. There, he befriended the composer David Amram who happened to raise a few milking goats.

"There it was, the milk just showed up!" says White, still incredulous at his good fortune. After making goat cheese for friends, word spread about his product. In 1993, White opened the Egg Farm Dairy in Peekskill and began to use cow's milk to make butter and aged cheeses.

Today, his cheese factory, a far cry from the cozy country farm, is a modern and efficiently organized industrial space. Behind his small retail shop, White stores his products in large refrigerated units. The rather sterile setting is deceptive, however. His creations, once served on the table, exude the complexity and richness of milk obtained only from grass-fed cows.

Since, according to White, "American butter lacks character," one of his primary goals in becoming a fromager was to put thick, yellow butter "back on the pedestal." To do so, he implemented traditional techniques of slightly souring the cream. While most commercial butters have a high concentration of water, White's butter is derived from a fourteen-hour cultured cream that is cooled before being churned. The effect is a warmer flavored product.

White also remembers that when he first opened his shop, he received valuable advice, much in line with his grandmother's teachings, from a baker who mused, "you can't learn to bake bread from a book, you can only learn it from the dough." Thus, White began experimenting, "to see what the cow's milk wants to do."

Cheese was just a hobby for Jonathan White (top right). The engineer became so consumed with the art that he eventually learned to create superb cheese products such as the Amram cheese (top left), named after a composer who first provided White with high-quality milk. Cheese is made out of milk's curd; using a large, screenlike sieve, White and his fellow cheese makers harvest it from giant vats (bottom). "It's like pushing jelly," White jokes.

White pasteurizes his milk at 145° for thirty "slow and gentle" minutes to ensure that the heated fluid maintains the qualities of crude milk. He then adds a small amount of rennet, an enzyme found in calves' stomachs, and lets the milk rest for twenty minutes until curd forms. Using a large screenlike sieve, White and his fellow cheese makers harvest the curd from giant vats. "It's like pushing jelly," he jokes.

White works with only two kinds of milk. The milk from the red Guernsey cow, while too rich for soft-ripened cheeses, is perfect for stirred curd cheeses. In contrast, milk from the European-breed Holstein cows, snow-white in color and lower in fat and protein than Guernsey milk, makes ideal soft-ripened cheeses.

Once the curd has been extracted from the milk, White lets the cheeses mold and age naturally. He explains that the sizes and shapes of cheeses "affect profoundly how they ripen." When the mold is filled with thin layers of curd, its geometry directs how the curd drains. Therefore, different shapes create different distributions of moisture. In turn, the moisture affects the ripening process—how and where the mold grows on the cheese surface.

For example, the small wheel-like Amram, named in honor of the milk-donating composer, is a wild, ripened cheese that releases a strong, vivid flavor. The larger Muscout cheese maintains a "firm but yielding" texture and pungent edge. Larger still, the Hudson, with a molten, creamy interior, bears the remote quality of "bittersweet chocolate." White loves the science of it. "I can have those three cheeses out there from within a week of each other in production -- same cow, same everything -- yet, they are completely different in flavor. And that's beautiful to me."

White, the modern cheese maker who still churns his butter by hand, likes to say that he has set the dairy industry back to the nineteenth century. That may be true, but it's all for the benefit of this century.

"With cow's cheese, just put it on a slice of good country bread simply toasted. Superb!"

JEAN-LOUIS PALLADIN

Fresh cheese

Milk, the symbol of vitality and growth, is the origin of all dairy products. Without premium milk, there is no cream, *crème fraiche*, butter, yogurt, or cheese worthy of expectant taste.

Two women, Sue Conley in California and Hallie Harron in Arizona, implement this simple motto in making fresh dairy foods. Conley runs the Cowgirl Creamery at the Tomales Bay Food Market in Point Reyes, California, and an artisan cheese store in San Francisco. Harron is a chef at The Farm at the South Mountain in Phoenix. Both depend on the highest-quality milk in creating superior fresh cheeses and butter.

Conley gets her organic milk from a nearby dairy farm, the Straus Creamery, located in a tumble of coastal hills in Marshall, California. In the late 1980s, upon quitting her restaurant business in Berkeley, she worked and trained with the dairy's owner, Albert Straus, for three years. During that time, Straus began to bottle the milk harvested from the 200 cows on his family farm. Today, Conley uses that same milk in her own products.

"Our cheese highlights the region's milk," Conley says, clearly pleased, while displaying her product line at the Tomales Bay Food Market. Across from her counter, Conley has set up a kitchen where she and her partner, Peggy Smith, make their fresh goods. An arrangement of clabbered cottage cheese, *crème fraiche*, "cooked at a low temperature for hours, it has a sweet, almond character," and *fromage blanc*, a white, yogurt-textured cheese, graces the shelves in simple invitation.

Conley has her own way to describe the 500 pounds of cheese she produces each week. "Each variety maintains the character of the milk I am using—fresh from open pastures, you can taste the grass. The flavor is also a little bit salty because there is sea salt in the air."

In an equally bucolic setting, down among the gardens of Phoenix, Harron similarly depends on exceptionally high-quality milk and cream. Working side by side with Italian-trained cheese maker, Carl Bonacci, Harron uses a "very pure" curd from New York to make a mozzarella wonderfully fresh, clean, and white.

"Making mozzarella seems very easy, but it's not. What you need is a very strong hand that can work in 170° water," Harron explains. Trained as a chef in France, Harron originally studied music, but recalls, "my piano teacher preferred my hors-d'œuvres to my Mozart."

Carefully dipping his hands into the boiling water, Bonacci works the curd sliced into thin pieces. Once submerged, the slices stretch slowly, as the outside layer heats more quickly than the interior one. The procedure must be done carefully, Bonacci warns with serious expression, noting that if the curd is

overworked, "it pushes all the fat out in the water." Once the mozzarella has expanded, it is placed in cold, unsalted water and within minutes the texture becomes firm.

Making butter is a slower process. Harron boasts that she serves only a solid, yellow, water-free butter and claims, "it's all heavy cream." Stirred with a special blender, the cream slowly thickens and expels the buttermilk, leaving behind a product with a luxuriant, rich texture. As a final touch, Harron adds Hawaiian sea salt. Wasting nothing, she makes *crème fraiche* from the residual buttermilk and cream.

While Harron's butter melts slowly and temptingly in the mouth, releasing waves of rich warmth, Conley's *crème fraiche* gives off a touch of nutty, delicate sweetness. Although both are derived from milk, the very distinct products are testament to two women, one from Arizona the other California, who have succeeded in making each of their creations a crowning regional specialty.

"There is nothing better than a warm summer salad of Maine lobster, tomatoes, and fresh mozzarella."

ALESSANDRO STRATTA

Fromage de chèvre

Goat cheese has come a long way in the United States. In the 1980s, most *chèvre* sold in the New York metropolitan area was imported from France. "And that," says cheese maker Miles Cahn, "was a stale cheese, several months old, which the dealer didn't know how to handle." Today, just two hours north of New York City, a dairy product can be found that is worlds away from the old French import. On his farm in Pine Plains, Cahn makes a cheese fresh enough to bear the authentic French appellation of *fromage de chèvre.*

Famous for having turned a small leather company into the international giant Coach Leather, Cahn and his wife, Lillian, originally from New York's Upper West Side, stumbled upon the scenic Upstate town in their search for a small weekend retreat. "It was a revelation, really," says Cahn. Inspired, the couple purchased a dairy farm and, remembering the high-quality chèvre they savored on their frequent trips to France, decided to transform it into a goat farm. "I thought," Cahn reminisces, "why couldn't we make it here and do the same thing?"

Yet, managing both the leather company and the goat farm proved more work than the couple had intended. "It was all naiveté." Cahn laughs. "What I wanted was a working farm that would give us a whole other thing to be occupied with. I wasn't looking to lie down in a hammock, but . . ." his voice tapers off. Lillian is more blunt, "we were nuts."

They sold their leather business and focused on the goat farm. Purchasing 200 Alpine breed goats, distinctive for their black-and-white coloring, the Cahns bequeathed the new place with their traditional logo, Coach Farm.

Within little time, Cahn learned several factors that would determine his success. In stark contrast to a cow's milk production, which can reach up to 100 pounds a day, goats produce an average of only five pounds of milk per day, with a maximum of seven. Moreover, those seven pounds of milk will yield less than one pound of cheese.

Cahn managed to increase the average milk production of his stock to seven pounds per animal. As he says, it took "a lot of genetics, good care, and good feed." Part of that good care is allowing the animals to roam freely in the open barns—eating and butting heads with surprising force and enthusiasm. The goats feed on only natural hay, which is grown on the farm's own 700-acre spread. Cahn supplements their diet with corn, oats, and soy to increase the nutritional value of the feed. "We have spoiled the goats," he confesses.

At the Coach Farm, located in Upstate New York, Miles Cahn (top right) makes his fresh goat cheese by hand. Under appreciated just a decade ago, goat cheese has become one of the country's most popular dairy products. Bearing names reminiscent of their shapes -- the Log, Disc, Medallion, Button, and Brick -- Cahn's cheeses have won several prizes at international expositions.

Upon opening the farm, Cahn employed the help of a French cheese maker, Marie-Claude Chaleix, who had bred goats in Bordeaux, France, and was in the practice of making artisanal cheeses. She instituted the farm's practice, now a tradition, of doing everything by hand. Cahn is clearly indebted, "we are making cheese the way Marie-Claude Chaleix did it in her kitchen, except that we pasteurize the milk."

The pasteurization process, which begins immediately after each milking, is done slowly and without the effect of dramatically high temperatures. The milk is then left to incubate overnight. The following day, the curd is hand-ladled into tapered molds where it drains for another twelve hours. Afterwards, the cheese is removed from the molds and salted. Rubbing his fingers together and sprinkling salt over the cheese with a twinkle in his eye, Cahn demonstrates, "this much." The final product is then packaged by hand, wrapped in a permeable paper that keeps the cheese "alive."

Beyond the picturesque setting, however, the Cahns also had to contend with marketing their product once the farm was set in motion. In 1988, with their first collection of fresh cheeses in hand, they entered a food exposition. Cahn enjoys recalling the public's initial response. "We put out our display—the very same signs and the same cheeses that we're making today. The crowd passed in droves and, as they went by, I saw them looking at our sign and heard them say, 'Yuck! Goat cheese.'"

Nevertheless, a few years later, one of his goat cheeses came to win first prize in an international competition. Following that, his series of hand-ladled cheeses, bearing names reminiscent of their shapes -- the Log, Disc, Medallion, Buttons, and Brick -- won the prize for outstanding product line. Not bad, Cahn admits, considering that twelve years earlier the cheese "had been a nothing."

In the nearby barn, a goat has just given birth to a wide-eyed, bleating kid. Cahn, looking amazed as if witnessing a birth for the first time, stares affectionately at the next member of his 1,000-goat herd. Maybe this one will give him eight pounds of milk a day.

"I savor goat cheese when it is not too dry and served at room temperature - sprinkled with a dash of olive oil, some thickly ground pepper and sel de Guérande (if the cheese is not already salted). I then dip bread in olive oil, and eat it along with the cheese."

ALAIN DUCASSE

FISH

Portland's Mayflower legacy

The office of Rod Mitchell, president and founder of Browne Trading Company in Portland, Maine, opens to a large wooden desk. Sitting straight in his chair behind the desk, Mitchell is a businessman. But tucked away in an adjacent room, among fishing rods and fisherman's clothes, hangs a photograph of the athletic man standing next to a six-foot marlin. Mitchell is a sportsman. There is no paradox, indeed the two sides blend into a man with impeccable knowledge of the sea. And no one has a better collection of its bounty than he.

Chefs from all over the country praise the quality marine products that Mitchell, through his wholesale company, has marketed over the years. "Excellent," "unparalleled," and "pristine" are a few of the adjectives consistently used. For there is good seafood and bad seafood, and not a lot in between. There are scallops hand-picked by scuba divers and those dragged from the bottom of the ocean. There are fish caught by hook and line and those by net. While some boats take care of their harvest, others are careless. According to Mitchell, while all these factors make the difference, the cost he may have to pay for that difference is irrelevant.

Indeed, Mitchell can spend $20 a pound to buy the best halibut of the day, or pay extra money to have men scuba dive for urchins in the freezing winter waters of the North Atlantic. The results are products served in the country's finest restaurants.

In a chic little bistro in the heart of Portland, Mitchell is served one of his freshly caught lobsters. Gently lifting a piece of velvety rose-colored meat on his fork, Mitchell steadily explains that he has continued a family tradition of fishing which, as if history bore no weight on him, originated at the time of the Mayflower. He speaks in a soft baritone tinged with nostalgia. "It was a time when America was young and when there was a lot of bounty and fish here."

Mitchell started fishing as a young boy with a minor obsession. His grandfather, Earl Browne, took him to Maine's Kennebec River and Casco Bay to teach him secrets of the skill. Smiling lightly, Mitchell remembers that he and his grandfather caught cod by the line very close to shore (something he admits is no longer possible due to the depletion of stock). At age seven, he caught his first big fish, an American striped bass. Enthralled, young Mitchell proceeded to catch every fish he possibly could: freshwater bass,

mackerel, flounder, and sole. His infatuation with the sea has not changed since, "every time I go fishing, I feel the same way, and I don't want to do anything else."

As an amateur fisherman, Mitchell always dreamed of combining his love for the sea with his professional life. While his career in food products began with a wine store he opened in Camden, Maine, his venture into the seafood business started the day he met Jean-Louis Palladin—at the time, the chef at *Jean-Louis* in Washington, D.C.'s Watergate Hotel. Upon visiting Mitchell's shop, the men struck up conversation and Palladin advised Mitchell to carry caviar along with his wine. Intrigued, Mitchell took the advice and soon found himself concentrating, inordinately, on his collection of the pearly roe. He closed the wine shop and began to sell only premium caviars, becoming a leading expert on the product in the process. Even today, Mitchell himself fills expensive boxes of the sturgeons' black eggs for his clients.

"Forget about the price," Mitchell bellows, leaning over the white-clothed dinner table, now sampling some of his lightly grilled scallops. "Is the caviar pleasant? Does it have a nice flavor? Think about all the effects of caviar." Although Mitchell first sold imported caviar from the Caspian Sea, he has since been instrumental in getting American caviar onto the market. Less expensive, American caviar is produced in California from farm-raised sturgeon. "Both carry the same qualities," Mitchell says, comparing the Russian to the American, "but their flavors differ because the fish grow in different waters and have a different diet."

Before long, Palladin began making rather exotic requests of Mitchell for other seafood products that he had a hard time finding for his restaurants, such as handpicked scallops and baby eels. The scallops that Palladin sought were not commonly found in the United States since, for economic reasons, most fishermen gather scallops by dragging nets across muddy ocean bottoms. Mitchell contends that during such practices, however, the scallops become stressed or, dumped on the boat's deck, often die from trauma. In contrast, when scuba divers pick the scallops up one by one in cold, winter waters, they are delicately placed into a bag, brought up to the boat, and immediately shucked on board. The muscle of the scallop, which has been promptly removed from the shell, is so fresh that, "snap it with your finger the next day and it will still be moving, keeping all that sweetness in."

Following the scallops, Mitchell began to market baby eels, known as "piballes," a delicacy from the rivers of Maine. The small, serpentlike animals are the offspring of the translucent glass eels and are widely recognized in France and Spain as a choice food. At Palladin's request, Mitchell decided to make them his catch. He designed a special net to snare the eels at the entrance of the rivers where the ocean's salt water flows into the fresh water. Available during the months of April and May, piballes can only be caught "when it's dark and the tide is very high." On spring evenings, Mitchell can be seen standing in the dark with net in hand, assisted solely by the glow of his flashlight, entrapping the small creatures.

Mitchell has always supported natural fishing methods. He prefers the hook to the net, believes that the time between catching and serving the fish must be kept to a minimum, and insists that fishermen handle fish one by one. "What makes somebody better at fishing is knowing what the fish are like," Mitchell says, sipping fine wine after his meal. "What do they do? What do they eat? Where do they live and when are they there? You have to know the fish to hunt them."

According to Mitchell, the superior quality of fish caught off the Maine coast is due primarily to the waters. The cold North Atlantic waters affect the beauty, the flavor, and the firmness of the fish. "The waters are cleaner, better," he says with honest expression. "Warm-water fish have a softer flesh and the meat texture is not as firm." In addition, Mitchell explains, the ocean circulation is different in the North Atlantic. "You have upwelling on this coast so you have many more nutrients on this side of the ocean." The result is a "very good diversity of fish," which are quite different from those caught in Pacific waters. The cod found off Maine, New Hampshire, and Massachusetts, "I would say are the best," Mitchell firmly states. He also catches monkfish, which swim in very deep cold waters, and skate (known as *raie bouclée* in France), which favor a flat, sandy bottom and "give a very nice white meat, not too bloody or muddy colored." However, he readily admits that the best wild salmon is found on the West Coast since the Atlantic wild salmon have been overfished nearly to the point of extinction.

Depending on the season, Mitchell sells between 50 to 75 different species brought back by the approximately 325 fishing boats that continuously land in Portland. While thousands of vessels used to dock in Portland, the government, in efforts to curb overfishing, bought hundreds of boats at prices far exceeding their value and reduced the fleet by two-thirds.

Nonetheless, Mitchell does not know all the fishermen and does not necessarily want to. "Everybody has a different kind of fishing," he says, and he avoids dealing with the fishermen who don't treat the catch well and then argue over prices at auction. When he does speak with fishermen, "I tell them what I expect. I tell them how to take care of their fish, how to make sure the fish stay perfect." The fishermen, Mitchell reasons, stand to profit if they take care of the fish, "because if I see it on the auction and it's what I want, I'll pay more money for it."

The harvesting methods used are the first indication of the caliber of the fish. The "hook-and-line" method is Mitchell's favorite. Pulled from the water alive, the fish is chilled immediately on the boat. Another method, which preserves most of the texture and flavor of the fish, is "dragging," or raking the bottom of the sea with a wide net. Mitchell approves of this method only as a way to gather certain fish and only when they are brought up to the boat within a few hours, still alive. The last, and most common method, which Mitchell does not approve of, is the use of a "gill net." Through this practice, a large net is kept in the water for several days. During such time, the fish are entangled in the net by their gill plates. They struggle, die, and are left in the water too long. "Fresh" fish, therefore, does not necessarily refer to fish brought straight from boat to market, but concerns the method of harvest as well.

Mitchell looks for certain characteristics of the fish in determining freshness: the clarity and color of the eyes, the firmness of the flesh, and the texture of the scales. In Maine, fishermen are not allowed to sell

directly to distributors such as Mitchell. All harvests must go through the auction market. Therefore, says Mitchell, "my job is to see who is coming and going from the port, and what is happening."

Mitchell's office, located on Commercial Street a block from the old port neighborhood and its narrow, granite streets, is next to the landing dock and the fish storage building. No one in town is in a better position to monitor boat traffic. If a boat stays off shore for three to five days, Mitchell knows that many of the harvested fish will not be fresh. "The most important thing to do is to get the fish to us as soon as possible, to take care of it, and to not let it freeze or get too warm."

Once the fish land in Portland, Mitchell reviews every load one by one and handpicks the specimens he wants. He then packages and ships the entire, untouched fish in special containers. He refuses to cut the fish into filets; in order to afford his clients the opportunity to inspect the product using their own methods, he sends the animal in its pristine state.

While seeking out fresh fish is Mitchell's passion, often waking at 3:00 A.M. to venture out into the sea with his fishing rod, he admits that his ultimate pleasure is simply eating his catches off the plate at the end of a long day. Much in the same manner his Mayflower ancestors most likely did at the end of their long days, passing on the fishing tradition.

"Crispy Monkfish Medallions: Cover the fish in plenty of cornmeal (or bread crumbs) with salt, pepper, and a bit of flour mixed with butter and olive oil. Grill it until light wisps of smoke appear. Shake off the monkfish, but don't turn it until it has browned. Serve with caper mayonnaise thinned with warm water and lemon juice."

DAVID GRANT

High bids by the sea

There is little danger that the small space will be mistaken for the auction room of Sotheby's or Christie's. It is cold, and men and women, uncomfortably seated in school-like chairs, quickly finish their lunches with cell phones in hand. They are all poised for the opening of the auction, not of fine art, but of the finest catches of the sea presented at the Portland Fish Exchange.

Steve Bowman, who works with Rod Mitchell at Browne Trading Company, sits in the second row. He knows exactly what he wants to buy. That morning, he and Mitchell had evaluated each lot of fish that would be offered at auction and ranked them according to quality and size. Now, Bowman patiently waits until the lot numbers he wants are called and he can begin bidding.

There is one, and only one, halibut he is eyeing. Bowman and Mitchell had inspected the 21-pound flat fish -- white on one side, brown on the other -- while making their rounds of the lot bins. "What makes Maine halibut so wonderful," Mitchell says of the fish caught in Alaskan as well as North Atlantic waters, "is its unique, fresh cucumber smell." While the fish to be auctioned is not as white as the Alaskan or Nova Scotian varieties, it retains a lovely, almost opaque quality. Bowman explains that halibut has been over-harvested and that "the stocks are down so the price is rising." Nonetheless, he will pay top dollar for a sleek, lustrous fish of similar quality to today's specimen. The skin, firm and unwrinkled, appears as if just pulled from the water. "This fish is no more than two days old," Bowman concludes, "we will definitely buy it."

Bidding on the halibut begins. Although it usually sells for no more than four to five dollars a pound, as bids continue the price quickly rises. Six, seven, eight, nine dollars . . . every contender has withdrawn except Bowman and another bidder. He leaves the room to call Mitchell, who has returned to his office, to see how high they will go. Prices go up—10, 11, 12, 13 dollars . . .

"Got to have it," shouts Joel Ray who, although not bidding himself on the halibut, watches with amusement the bidding parlay. Bowman doesn't laugh, he is intent on winning the fish. "This is a record!" Ray cries. At $20 a pound, bidding stops. Bowman has won the halibut for a total price of $420.

"That halibut was top of the line," Ray says, clearly impressed, noting that it is a rare fish for December. Indeed, Mitchell later learned from the fisherman who had caught the prize halibut that no fewer than 50 halibuts had actually been pulled onto his boat that day. According to the law, however, only one such fish per boat per day is allowed into port for sale.

Looking for the best halibut of the day (top left)—or is that a monkfish (top right)?—Steve Bowman (top left) wanders around the alleys of the Portland Fish Exchange. Earlier in the night, dozens of boats docked and delivered their catch. Distributors like Bowman take note of the many fish that might interest their customers. They inspect the fish, touch them, scrutinize the color of the irises, and finally decide how much they are willing to pay for them. A few hours later, they gather to bid for their chosen lots.

Between 60 and 80 fishing vessels had arrived at 4:00 A.M. in the middle of a long, cold December night to deliver their harvests. As most mornings, once the boats unload, Rick Whitten, who works for the Portland Fish Exchange, sorts the fish out by species and size. Buyers such as Mitchell then come into the storage area and inspect each lot, one by one. Carefully, they select the products upon which they will bid, marking the sizes and weights in their notepads.

Bowman stops by a wolffish lot and picks one up. He likes the color of the eyes' irises, "that fish was probably caught yesterday." He inspects another, which is very firm and, therefore fresh, but undersized. He freely admits that he learned everything from Mitchell, whom he describes as, "very discriminating about what he wants, and if you get it wrong, you are going to hear about it."

To discern the freshest fish, "the trick is in the eye and in the hand," Mitchell says simply. "Look at the cod," he points to an animal found in Maine waters at depths of 100 to 200 feet. "It is soft, the color of the skin is not nice, and the eye is white, still clear, but not perfect," Mitchell concludes. The men look exclusively for animals with luminous scales, "luster also indicates freshness."

A note attached to each lot provides information on the fish and its provenance. "Looking at the original boat can save you time because you know the boats that don't harvest good fish," Bowman, himself familiar with the crews and their fishing practices, says. "It's a matter of handling the fish, of gutting it out in a timely fashion, of cleaning it up, and of conserving it."

Wandering down the rows of fish in the storage area, Bowman discovers some nice dabs, known also as lemon sole. However, the hake he sees, which, to retain the ideal firmness should not be out of the water for more than twelve hours, does not please him.

Nonetheless, "everything will be sold," Bowman explains. His company will pay the fishermen more to get the best lots. "Middle guys buy the bulk," he adds. And the remaining fish will be sold very cheaply. As in life, there are high bidders, low bidders, and those who make the lucky catch.

"Cook the halibut briefly in the oven with pepper and sea salt, but serve it almost raw."

ERIC RIPERT

Florida fish

Gary Reed, a founder and owner of Gary's Seafood in Orlando, Florida, remembers the day he invited a group of top chefs out fishing. Cruising into a school of tuna, the men baited their hooks and cast them into the water. They stood relaxed and chatting, expecting an easy day of fishing. After a few minutes, one chef felt a tug on his fishing rod. As he began to pull in the line, with a sudden "twang," the entire fishing rod flew from his hand and, arching high into the air, splashed into the water far from the boat. Stunned, the chef had had no concept of the fish's strength. When the men hauled in their last load of fish, the $800 fishing rod surfaced, tangled with the final tuna. That day, the chefs learned the real cost of freshness: hard work.

In the early 1980s, Reed, his wife, Lorraine, and his friends Mitch Rice and Brad Weiss, launched their seafood company in Orlando to distribute the best and most unusual fish caught in the warm Florida waters.

"I've always fished," Reed says. "Ever since I could ride a bicycle, I'd ride to the ocean and fish." Continuing his hobby throughout his life, he later graduated from a bicycle to a specially designed mobile processing unit to start a commercial business. Without access to a warehouse which could handle his dozens of freshly hooked and netted snappers and groupers, he conceived of the mobile unit as the fastest way to get the products from the water to the restaurants. "My wife thought that I was crazy, that we were going to go broke," he says laughing lightly, "but it turned around and worked out very well."

While he began selling grouper and snapper, two of the most commonly caught fish in the area, Reed quickly decided to enter the market of wider, more exotic varieties. Today, his stock, selectively gathered from local fishermen, includes pompano, escolar, tilefish, swordfish, and the Key West yellowtail snapper. According to Reed, three of the fish he offers stand out for their excellence: the wahoo, the hogfish, and the cobia.

The long, slender wahoo, identifiable by stripes along its sides, swims in small groups of two to three and is found in warm seas extending from Florida down to Venezuela. Extraordinarily difficult to catch, it can be a rare market product. Even rarer is Brad Weiss's favorite, the hogfish. "Its face just looks like a hog," he bluntly describes, "but its snow-white meat has an extremely delicate flavor." According to Weiss, the hogfish's uniquely elegant texture results from the fish's discerning diet of shrimp and lobster. A large animal, with an average weight of six pounds, the hogfish often eludes hook-and-line techniques and is usually seized by traps or spears. "It's hit or miss," Weiss admits.

The cobia, Rice's favorite, is much larger and, according to many, a frightening fish. Also known as the lemon fish, the cobia can reach 100 pounds and has a tremendous, gaping mouth. "It's got a meat all of its

The team at Gary's Seafood (top left) enjoy putting unusual fish on the market, in addition to the more common snappers and groupers. The long, slender wahoo, the rare hogfish, and the frightening cobia top a lengthy list of exotic fish. Off the coast of Florida, sharks are also a desirable catch. Joe Ludwig (right) makes his living by pursuing the legendary dagger-toothed animal. While displaying his bait, he likes to tell the story of an 1,800-pound mako shark—a powerful creature that managed to escape Ludwig's hook (bottom left).

own," says Rice, describing the cobia's firm, dark flesh. Like the wahoo and the hogfish, the cobia is also a hard catch, but for the specific reasons of its overbearing size and tendency to swim close to shore under the cover of reefs and shipwrecks.

Beyond their natural practice of handling the fish carefully, the men also know that restaurants pay for an excellent harvest. "We demand the best from fishermen," Reed explains. "If it's not good, we return it. And the fishing houses know it—they know we have a very tough back door."

John Polston, owner of King's Seafood of Port Orange, Florida, passed that door. His fleet of 60-foot vessels which venture out at night cast between 500 and 700 hooks and release 25 miles of line. From his store, located on the dock of the port, Polston has a clear view of the boats entering and leaving the port. Almost more importantly, he knows all the fishermen on his boats and is confident in their professional harvesting practices.

One of Polston's specialties, among the many varieties of fish he provides Reed, is the orange swordfish which, as its name indicates, bears a vibrant pumpkin-colored meat. A large and aggressive animal, it can only be caught by hook and line during the summer months before it mysteriously disappears in October for the remainder of the year.

According to Reed, the swordfish, along with pompano, can be one the most expensive fish on the market. Since the swordfish is an endangered species, he reports that the supply simply cannot meet the demand any longer. On any given expedition, a boat can sail back to port with a catch of only ten fish. Often, it returns with none.

Another animal caught by hook and line, and with significant courage, is the shark. Joe Ludwig, who sails off of Port Orange, makes his living in pursuit of the legendary dagger-toothed creature. Sharks are found virtually anywhere off the Florida coast and, of all fish, they can be the most dangerous catch. Not, however, while the animal is in the water. Occasionally, when the dead shark is hauled aboard the boat, the animal's still-functioning nervous system will trigger the powerful jaws to snap violently. Anyone standing near the animal, Ludwig warns, risks losing a limb.

Using hundreds of hooks baited with smaller sharks, Ludwig pulls tiger sharks, sandbar, and mako sharks onto his 36-foot boat. His favorite, the sandbar shark, bears high-quality meat and first-grade fins which are keenly popular in the Asian market for soups.

Ludwig recalls, with obvious liking of his trade, the biggest shark he ever encountered—an 1,800-pound mako. Pointing to the entire length of the boat, he estimates the size of the fish. "His tail was by the stern of the boat, and his head reached up to the Captain's chair," Ludwig laughs incredulously. "In the struggle, it got away."

According to Ludwig, the shark population has declined in the last ten years. "They changed their habits. In the past, we could go 15 miles in any direction from the inlet to find some. Now, we have to sometimes travel up to 60 miles. They are using different migration 'highways' and changing depths."

Far from the sharks and deep seas, the inner-coastal waterways flowing down to Miami carry a delicate fish with a rather courtly name, the pompano. Feeding on mainly crab and shrimp, the fish has a high oil content and firm, tan-colored meat that Reed describes as a delicacy.

A seafood expert in his own right, Reed elaborates on all the varieties he catches: the snowy grouper, found in deep seas, bears a delicate, almost sweet flavor; the black grouper, yielding a red meat, has a more complex texture; the tilefish, commonly caught in deep craters at the bottom of the ocean, is known as the "poor man's lobster" and offers a white, tender meat.

When asked his choice if only one fish could be kept from a day's lot, Reed responds, without hesitation, "the Key West yellowtail snapper!" A fast-moving fish, it eludes the hook and line. For that very challenge, Weiss and Rice pursue it as a hobby. "We let the bait drift back, and the fish come up and hit it," Reed explains. Although patience and dedication are required, the delicate, light and buttery taste of the fish is worth the sweat expended in the catch.

The men of Gary's Seafood, whose livelihood focuses on the breaking dawn hours when fishing boats sail into port, live by that tenacious sense of dedication. As the chef who lost his fishing rod in the seas could tell them, freshness requires hard work.

"The smaller the pompano, the more delicate the flavor."

ALESSANDRO STRATTA

Salmon's kingdom

A few houses stretch along the misty coastline and snowcapped mountains dangle cliffs overhead. In the harbor, bald eagles rest atop high-masted troll boats. Apart from the 8,500 inhabitants of Sitka, a small city once the Russian capital of Alaska, and two other small communities, no one else lives on Baranof Island. Yet, in the summer, when the sun beats out the clouds and rain in rare conquest, tourists suddenly appear. Nearly all of them come to fish the king salmon. Isolated in the southeastern Alaskan wilderness, Sitka is a sanctuary for the largest and the most complex of all the wild salmon.

"King salmon are the reason why the Tinglits Indians came to Sitka," says Isabella Brady, a native Alaskan and member of the Tinglit tribe. "Fishing was a year-round activity." Hundreds of years later, salmon remains at the core of Sitka's economy, local culture, and diet. Almost 50 percent of the population makes a living, directly or indirectly, from fishing. Before the advent of airfreighting in the late 1970s, the only Alaskan king salmon to be found outside of Alaskan waters was either smoked, canned, or frozen. Today, fresh salmon is enjoyed across the world.

"I understand the responsibility we have with these wonderful wild creatures that are giving their lives to sustain us," explains Eric Jordan, one of the 188 troll salmon permit holders in Sitka, as well as a member of several marine conservation organizations. "It's our responsibility to share the earth with them." While the hook-and-line fishing methods employed to catch the great salmon preserve the fish's natural qualities, the well-organized conservation efforts behind the local fishing industry preserve the animal's habitat and chances of survival.

King salmon, also known as chinook salmon, dominates its cousins -- the coho, sockeye, chum, and pink salmon -- in physique and instinct. After hatching in a freshwater river, the king salmon travels to the ocean to begin a seven-year, lifelong journey. A journey that will end when the fish becomes sexually mature and returns to the river where it was born to spawn, give life anew, and then die.

"It's a magnificent fish," says Jordan. "The tastiest, the sweetest, and richest fish around, king salmon gathers the plankton and the bounty of the ocean and brings them back to us."

"The king salmon is out in the ocean, swimming and running and working hard to get itself something to eat," echoes Bob Schell, a former teacher turned fisherman and member of a board of directors for one of Sitka's two salmon processing plants. "It's the most oily of the salmon."

Waves are high and it is already late morning. Birds are flying low over the surface of the choppy water, indicating the presence of small fish that the king salmon feed on. Suddenly, Dan Stockel (top right) announces a catch and starts reeling in his line. The excitement of the first catch of the day fills the boat, but not for long. The large specimen, a real fighter, breaks away from the hook and swims back to the depths of the Pacific.

The rich meat, either red or white in color -- depending on the genetic disposition of the fish and its diet -- results from the thousands of miles the powerful fish has swum throughout the North Pacific in its lifetime.

Due to its incomparable nature, the salmon is not an easy fish to catch. And preserving the richly textured meat requires absolute care of the animal from the time it is pulled aboard the ship until the time it is carried into the kitchen.

In Alaska, troll fishing is permitted only in the southeastern reaches of the sea—from northern Cape Suckling down to the Canadian border. The cold waters are preferable to the warmer temperatures found along the continental Pacific coastline in large part because the "upwelling, due to the cold Japanese currents of the Sitka coastline, brings more nutrients to the fish," explains Dan Stockel, president of Alaska Hook & Line Seafoods, Inc., a Sitka-based distribution company specializing in sales of North Pacific fish. Troll fishing, the superior method for catching salmon, involves boats equipped with multiple weighted lines of hooks and bait that are towed through deep waters. In contrast to nets, the quick catch made by hook and line prevents bruising and suffocation of the animal. Although troll fishing typically promises higher-quality fish, high seas and stormy weather can make it a dangerous practice.

Born into a fishing family in 1949, Jordan was only seven months old when his parents first brought him onto a boat. He knows many key secrets to catching the king salmon, primarily, locating the fish and getting it to bite. Almost solitary, the king salmon is difficult to spot because it doesn't swim in schools and continuously changes its swimming patterns. To locate the salmon, Jordan first looks for the smaller fish they feed on, such as herring, squid, and needlefish. Once offshore, he searches the horizon for sea ducks, cormorants, and other birds that often signal the presence of these smaller fish. Spotting salmon is often the easiest in spring, during the herring spawning season when huge schools of herring, extending nearly 60 miles, attract the salmon. These seasonal feeding patterns, which include winter migrations of squid, also affect the ultimate taste of the salmon.

On this late April morning, Jordan stares at his sonar. There are one or two salmon that appear as small blips on the screen. But it's already late, past 10:00 A.M., and the salmon are less likely to take the bait. "They bite best at dawn and at dusk, when there is a change of light happening," he explains. A large fish -- the biggest catch recorded weighed in at 126 pounds -- "they fill themselves up just like a lion." Obviously impressed, Jordan says that the salmon will eat vast amounts at one time before it stops feeding altogether for a digesting period that can last for days.

"When you are at your top level as a fisherman, it goes beyond the craft and the hard work," Jordan says. "You're in tune with what's happening to the point that it becomes an extrasensory artistic experience."

Still, the fisherman must be well-equipped. Choosing the right kind of lure, either a painted plastic squid (called a hootchie), a spoon (which flashes in the water in imitation of an injured fish), or a fake squirming fish, can make the difference in hooking a great catch. Yet, once a king salmon has bitten, the real battle begins. Standing on his 38-foot boat, barehanded after a king salmon managed to escape from his hook,

Jordan compliments the fish's fighting instinct. "They jump and run and do everything they can to get off the hook," he says. Once a fish surfaces, every aspect of a fisherman's dexterity comes into play.

Using a gaff hook, made out of a long piece of wood, Jordan kills the fish instantly with a single, swift stroke to the head. "Then I gently pull it aboard," Jordan says, adding that he makes sure not to bruise the animal. The animal is then bled, gutted and cooled in 29° iced saltwater from the ocean. "To me," Jordan concludes, "that process is the key to the high quality."

"Afterwards, there is a clock ticking on that fish," adds Joe Dalton, sales manager of Alaska Hook & Line. A king salmon properly handled and iced has a shelf life of six to ten days after capture.

Brought to port the day of the catch, the fish are immediately graded and processed in one of the two plants in town. Some fishermen, including Randy and Carolyn Nichols, live on their boats. Sailing with their children for two-week periods, the couple freezes their harvests on board—maintaining the pristine quality of the meat. Dalton and his partner, Stockel, choose some of the best cuts to be shipped nationwide from the airport only one mile away. Many fishermen and fish processors in Sitka don't approve of the antics of the sellers at Seattle's famous market. Throwing the salmon about in entertaining display to amuse buyers, the sellers often bruise the animals and compromise the efforts of the fishermen.

Although the North Pacific king salmon has inspired the reputation of fine fishing in Alaskan waters, it remains a rare treat. Due to the limited king salmon population, restrictions are placed on the number of fish that can be caught. The 1999 Pacific Salmon Treaty -- a wide-standing agreement between fisherman from Alaska, Washington State, and Canada -- limited the fishing of king salmon to about 195,600, all commercial and sports methods included. Thus, out of the almost one hundred million salmon fished in southeast Alaska in 1999, either by troll or net, only 132,800 were trolled king salmon which could be placed on the market. And while another 12,900 king salmon were net fished, 47,400 were claimed by sports fishermen.

In addition, the commercial fishing of troll-caught king salmon is limited to precisely defined seasons. Winter and spring range from mid-October to mid-April, and summer extends from early May to mid-July, although fisheries sometimes remain open for a few days in late August and September.

"Fishermen spend a lot of time without pay serving on boards and commissions that help regulate the fisheries," explains Deborah Lyons, a fisheries consultant. "The preservation of sustainable stock is our very first priority." Another famous catch of southeast Alaska is the giant halibut, the cheeks of which are delicacies. "It has a crab texture," describes Dalton, "with a delicate and sweet fishy flavor." Rockfish, black cod (or sablefish), shrimp, crab, and herring complete the fishing harvest.

Jordan, whose record catches -- made through three separate days of fishing -- include 1,300 chums, 812 cohos, and 150 kings, recognizes that king salmon have been more abundant in the two last decades.

"The ocean habitat is very healthy for salmon, especially off the coast of Alaska," he points out. The lush Sitka spruce trees lend an immaculate, deep green color to the Tongass National Forest surrounding Baranof Island. Deer frequently swim in the ocean waters between islands and bears prowl along river banks searching for salmon.

Problems arise with the conditions of the rivers, however, closer to Canada, Washington, and Oregon, where the water can be exposed to denser pollution.

"We have learned that salmon are not compatible with urban development," Jordan states. "We have to take care of them in the freshwater spawning habitat." Dams, mining runoff, clear-cut forestry, road pavement, and hydro power have all changed the quality of the water. "As a troller [fisherman], the demise of this wonderful way of life is the loss of the habitat for the king salmon in Canada and the continental 48 states."

The modern practice of reproducing salmon in a hatchery environment before introducing them into the immense ocean doesn't comfort Jordan. "We don't understand enough about the biology of the creature to maintain a genetic diversity resistant to disease."

But in southeast Alaska, king salmon continue to populate the waters where local residents and fishermen persist in braving the dismal weather, the winds, and waves to catch the fish.

Aside from the loss of habitat and corresponding decline in the wild salmon population, Jordan fears "the magic" of fishing could someday be lost. In the meantime, after a day on the water, where his expertise and intuition have guided him well in hooking many king salmon, Jordan joins his friends at the Pioneer Bar. Facing the harbor, the place is warm and intimate with the camaraderie of fishermen. A large bell above the wooden bar waits to be rung by the holder of the day's biggest catch, beckoning people throughout the port to come around for a drink.

"Prepare the King salmon raw and very thinly sliced. Serve it with olive oil and a lemon juice."

ERIC RIPERT

FRUIT

Meyer lemon and other citrus

A hint of lemon, a hint of mandarin, or is it sweet orange? Biting into a succulent slice of the Meyer lemon, one ponders these questions while enjoying the surprising tangy-sweet sensation. Lemon shaped and saffron colored as a young fruit budding on the tree, once ripe, it becomes a deep orange yellow. And while the golden flesh has some acidity, the mild bitterness is complemented by a sweet floral bouquet. The truth is, the Meyer lemon is a hybrid of a lemon and an orange or mandarin.

For all the complexity that makes the Meyer lemon such a wonder, it also makes it a mystery. Once overlooked in California's backyards, today it holds high rank in the kitchens of top chefs across the United States. "California likes to claim the Meyer lemon as its own," says Michael Foskett, president of California Citrus Specialties. But the fruit's history is more exotic.

In the early 1900s, a botanist named Franck Meyer brought a citrus from China to the United States which he believed was a hybrid of a lemon and a mandarin. Its tree, hardier than other lemon trees, adapted perfectly to the California climate. While the fruit enjoyed an initial popularity and was grown in backyards for its ornamental appeal, the Meyer lemon, despite its touch of sweetness, received little attention in the public culinary eye.

"I don't think that people had the sophistication of our palate at that time, and the chefs weren't out there the way they are today," explains Foskett, who commercially grows no fewer than 18 varieties of citrus fruits in California's Central Valley. "Now they find that the aromatic zest from this citrus really adds a lot of flavor."

The Meyer lemon is just one of the dozens of varieties of citrons, lemons, mandarins, oranges, and grapefruits that grow in America's southern regions extending east from California to the southern states bordering the Gulf of Mexico. Originally cultivated in Southeast Asia, citrus fruits were praised for their fragrant aromas and brilliant, delicate blossoms. From the East, the fruits were brought to Persia and Europe in 300 B.C., long before they were introduced to America by Columbus in the late fifteenth century. Even once landed on American soil, it took nearly three centuries and the Spanish colonization before actual orchards of orange trees appeared in California.

Today, with its warm summer days and cool winter evenings, the California Central Valley, which Foskett calls "the citrus belt of California," nurtures one of citrus's most resplendent fruits: the blood orange. Just days before Christmas, the first crop of sanguine-colored oranges is ready to be picked and used

From the uniquely sweet Meyer lemon to the bizarre-looking Buddha's Hand citron, dozens of fruits belong to the citrus family. Each is different in shape, peel, color, and taste. But the favorite of Michael Foskett (right), a citrus grower in California's Central Valley, remains the Page mandarin. The seedless fruit resembles an orange and, as Foskett explains, "it has the sweetest flavor and is a very durable piece of fruit."

for the festivities. "What it takes in the wintertime are these good cold snaps to bring the flavor in and the color up in the fruit," Foskett explains.

Foskett grows three varieties of blood oranges: the moro, the egg-shaped sanguinelli, and the tarocco. The moro, with its deep crimson color, is a favorite among chefs, although Foskett favors the tarocco, a richly flavored Italian variety. According to him, the deep raspberry and strawberry overtones of the tarocco blend well with the page mandarin to make a crisp drink. He picks up a sliced half of tarocco dripping scarlet colored juice, "you can squeeze the blood orange on top of the page and it floats!"

This may explain why the page mandarin happens to be Foskett's favorite, "it has the sweetest flavor and is a very durable piece of fruit." Bearing characteristics of the more rugged regular mandarin, the page mandarin, typically seedless, resembles an orange. "It has a distinctive little circle around the bottom, at the flower end of the fruit," explains Foskett. "It's like a little belly button."

Foskett, and his partner, Lance Walheim, author of a thorough guide on growing citrus, have maintained a keen interest in introducing new citrus varieties to the American public, some of them not so easily harvested. An example, the Kieffer lime, highly valued in Thai cuisine for its heavy oil content, grows behind a cluster of thorns, each of which extends up to two and one-half inches.

Of all the members of the citrus family, the Buddha's Hand citron holds the most exotic appeal. Resembling long, bony fingers, the fruit's appendages grow out and together like clasped hands poised in prayer. In the fourth century B.C., monks from Tibet allegedly brought the Buddha's Hand citron along the Yangtze Valley as an offering to the golden Buddhas found in regional Chinese temples. Like all citron, the Buddha's Hand citron has a thick, aromatic rind, but little pulp or juice. With an incredibly potent fragrance, it is perfect for zesting.

With its warm climate, open orchards, and ample sun, California boasts the best of the Asian treasures which, brought over for their delicate blossoms centuries ago, provide the richest and sweetest juices in America today.

"Cut the Meyer lemon into thick slices, add salt and pepper, and stuff them into a striped bass flavored with dried fennel. Grill it over open fire."

LAURENT MANRIQUE

Dates, Jordan in California

A gorge in southern California known as Coachella Valley, west of Palm Springs, is so hot and dry throughout the year that it likens to a Jordanian desert. Located below sea level, the parched air and scorching sun create the ideal conditions to yield a perfect date. Perhaps for this reason, you'll find little else but the wide-sweeping palm leaves of date trees in Coachella Valley.

The date is indigenous to North Africa and the Middle East, where the sun, soil, and water swirl together to create virtual forests of date palms. Indeed, the names of each variety of date lends an exotic quality, as well as distinct personality, to the vibrant, viscous fruit: the Deglet Noor, the soft and moist Medjool, the tender and firm Barhi, the black Dayri, and the crunchy Zahidi.

"The Barhi, which I discovered in Iraq, is the most erotic date," says Robert Lower, a date grower in Coachella Valley, while selling his fruits at the San Francisco farmer's market. "Women love it because it is a smooth and very sensual date," he says with sly expertise as though sharing a valuable secret.

Dates were brought to California in 1910 and thrived under the western sun. Since dates require a combination of dry weather and at least two thousand hours of 100° weather per year, Coachella Valley is a consummate location to harvest large, healthy crops.

Although Lower started growing dates in the mid-1970s at his Flying Disc Ranch, he first became enthralled with the nearly iridescent fruit while traveling through Turkey, Lebanon, and Egypt. Currently residing in Coachella Valley, Lower has succeeded in enhancing the natural qualities of his ranch by growing his fruits, as he says, biodynamically.

"Everything starts with water, soil, and sun; biodynamic cultures get the best of these three elements."

Lower never cultivates his soil. "If the land were to be opened, the sunlight would kill its fertility." Therefore, to enhance the soil's performance, Lower adds up to 20,000 pounds of compost to each acre, using grass, sticks, and chicken manure from the ranch. The compost effectively preserves the organisms and nutrients existing underground while, at the same time, protecting them from the sun's ultraviolet rays. On the other hand, the dates themselves need strong doses of sunshine. To maximize the drying effect of the sun, Lower places crystals on the ground and within the trees to reflect and magnify the light.

"The rest of the growing process on the ranch remains perfectly natural," Lower says unequivocally.

That's not to say that this natural process doesn't pose hazards to the date farmer. The Flying Disc Ranch harbors snakes that find refuge under the wide palm leaves and slink around the bases of the trees.

At the San Francisco farmer's market, Robert Lower, who harvests dates in the hot Coachella Valley, takes the time to discuss the growing process of his fruits with customers. Lower takes great pleasure in describing the many varieties. With a smile, he offers some secrets on the date. "The Barhi, which I discovered in Iraq, is the most erotic date," he asserts. "Women love it because it is a smooth and very sensual date."

Yet, as deadly as they can be, snakes balance a healthy ecosystem. Along with birds and cats, "they keep control of the small mammals, which are a real threat to the fruits," Lower says, adding that he kills the snakes only when their numbers get alarmingly high.

The same quality control applies to spiders and toads, which, by praying on large and harmful pests, allow the small, beneficial insects to survive. "The motto," Lower says, "is the more insects per square foot, the less infection per pound."

He readily acknowledges that the surrounding wildlife plays a large role in bringing out the best dates. So much so, that Lower refuses to use any sort of pesticide, which he believes "would be detrimental to the trees and the fruits themselves."

Ironically, the greatest obstacle in gathering the dates that have developed well over the course of the season is the tree itself. Harvest runs from September to November, with the exception of certain varieties, such as the Dayri, which require two extra months of growing time. To reach the fruits, Lower has to maneuver around two-inch long, knife-shaped thorns that jut out along the entire length of the tree trunk, which usually averages a height of 25 feet. Undaunted, Lower scales the trees and skillfully cuts the fruits from the branches. He then separates the crops and adds water to the dates before letting them dry under the California sun.

Although Lower literally goes to great heights to gather his prized dates, a look of bliss comes over his face as he bites into one of his tender specimens. He looks around artfully—if asked, he just may share one of the date's many savory secrets.

"Open the dates from the side, remove the pits, fill them with marzipan flavored with either kirsh or rum, and roll them in crystal sugar."

SYLVAIN PORTAY

Bursting berries

The road from Joe Mello's suburban neighborhood, south of San Jose, California, leading to the West Coast, turns continuously through sculpted canyons before breaking over the mountains. Dipping down toward the ocean, a breathtaking view of green berry fields, stretching wide across Pajero Valley, gracefully appears.

Mello, founder of Green Valley Specialty Farms, which grows and distributes berries across the country, once had a dream of the perfect raspberry. A raspberry that would grow soft and ripe as other varieties slipped into off-season dormancy. While working at the research department for Reiter Berry Farms, Mello, with the help of Dr. Stephen Wilhem, created a raspberry that was impervious to the isolated Pajero Valley winter. Locked between the ocean and the mountains, "it can be freezing out here," says Mello of the valley, "but the 'Joe Mello Berry' keeps producing."

At seventy-three, Mello, who has retired from big production farming and now farms only 50 acres of superior berries, waxes nostalgic about his fruits. "It's one of the things that I've done in my life that I am the most proud of."

Mello grows only a little of the best on his narrow plot of land: the blackberry, a complex potent fruit with a touch of bitterness, is best tamed in jams or sweet pies; the blueberry, with its velvety plumpness, has to be protected with netting from covetous birds; raspberries, tender little bubblelike sacs of juice, pop sweetness in the mouth; currants, small smooth globes provide a bittersweet bite; and elderberries, "good for the prettiest jams and jellies," also make a sweet wine, Mello says.

Among the 30 varieties he grows, Mello's favorite pome, small and hidden under clusters of verdant leaves, is the delicate French wild strawberry, or the *fraise des bois*.

Although the strawberry is highly perishable and requires particular care, Mello dismisses the effort as a small price to pay for its unique taste. "We brought the seed back from France," he explains. "We planted them here, and because the climate is so good . . .." The farmer does not finish his sentence. There is little point. One breath of the strawberry's honey-sweet perfume speaks for itself. Mello, who admits he was "suprised" to provide upscale chefs with his fruits, is not prone to needless conversation. Instead, he slides his hand under the diminutive leaves and picks up one, two, three wild strawberries. White or red, the heart-shaped fruits are full of cloying juices.

"Just give them a lot of water, especially the day before they are picked," Mello generously explains, "it takes a lot of patience, though." The patience of handpicking berries ten months out of the year, which is celebrated the instant a fruit is slipped onto the tongue.

"Prepare the wild strawberries with crème fraiches, sugar, lime juices, and nothing else."

JEAN-LOUIS PALLADIN

Apricots and cherries versus Silicon Valley

Despite common belief, Silicon Valley's richest resource is not the computer chip, but a medley of ruby-red cherries and coral-colored apricots. Long before computer technology stormed into central California in the early 1970s, fruit trees reigned peacefully over Sunnyvale, a small city south of San Francisco. Today, housing developments, ushered in by the corresponding economic boom, creep relentlessly over the horizon like swarming bees. While apricot and cherry trees still stand, like solitary soldiers in defensive posture, it is clearly a battle to survive in Silicon Valley, where land has become some of the most expensive in the United States.

According to one farming family, the Olsons, who have harvested California fruit for nearly a century, one acre of land in Silicon Valley is worth one million dollars. At the same time, raising and processing apricots and cherries in the area is not cheap. Handpicked, the apricots, processed into dried apricots, cost $2.50 a pound to produce before they even reach the market. While not as expensive to produce, the cherry harvest, nonetheless, has declined greatly since the onset of urban sprawl. In 1999, the cherry and apricot crop dropped to 1,100 pounds—a mere 22 percent of the 25,000 tons that were harvested in the 1930s and 40s. Indeed, much has changed since those early years.

When the Olson family settled in Sunnyvale in 1900, the area was known as the "Valley of Heart's Delight." In the spring, a hike up the nearby mountains provided a spectacular view of the glen's white- and rose-colored cherry, plum, and apricot blossoms.

Enticed by a newspaper advertisement promising "a train trip, a free barbecue, and generous terms for the purchase of property in Sunnyvale," the Olson family arrived ready to start business. They promptly bought five acres, built a modest house, and in 1902, planted their first cherry orchard. By 1935, the Olsons were selling their products from a fruit stand on the busy street corner of El Camino Real, and fostering a reputation for having the freshest, ripest fruits in the area.

Today, Deborah Olson, who is in charge of the family's four-generation business (the stand has now expanded into a store), still puts up colorful, handwritten signs offering fruits full of flavor and color. Most passersby, including a number of loyal customers who have been coming for years, are lured in and stop to sample the fruits. Olson remains modest, "this area is known for its fruits because of the microclimate and the fertile soil."

WORLD'S

Olson was born in 1957 in the last part of May, fittingly, at the peak of the cherry season. As though the particularly good crop that year announced her legacy, Olson has carried on her family's one-hundred-year tradition of farming fruit. Beginning at age six, Olson worked side by side with her grandmother, Rose, before she started to accompany her father on trips selling their prized Bing cherries—particularly sweet, they fetched the highest prices. As a young adult, she moved to France to study cooking. During her training with various famous chefs, she received a call from her grandmother. "Come home. The cherry season has started, and we need you," Olson remembers the message. "So," she concludes phlegmatically, munching on some of her dried apricots, "the next day, I got on a plane and came back."

When Olson took over the family store on El Camino Real in the mid-1980s, the shed was open only during the short growing season, extending from mid-May to the end of June. Wanting to expand her correspondingly short market season, Olson began to seek out premium cherries from other nearby farmers. "I just started fixing up the place," Olson explains. Yet, despite her efforts, she was unable to bear the cost of the family's entire legacy and the Olsons made the difficult decision to sell a few plots of their land to local developers.

According to Suzi Blackman, President of the Chamber of Commerce of Sunnyvale, there are fewer than 20 acres of orchards remaining in Sunnyvale. She reports that local residents are of two minds: that the trees are the community's heritage, or that the land should be used to accommodate commercial expansion. "Fifty years ago, the valley was covered with orchards" Blackman explains. "We have to preserve more of the orchards, because once they're gone, they're gone forever."

Despite the evident threat, the six varieties of cherries and the Blenheim apricots that the Olsons grow stand in beautiful rebellion to the mounting concrete and highways.

Among the rows of chocolate-covered apricots and cherries in her store, Olson grabs a handful of walnuts that she buys from nearby Stockton, California. "Look at them, they are fantastic." Using her fingers, she cracks the nut, freeing two perfectly shaped halves into her palm. She pops one into her mouth, "they have an unbelievable taste," she says with palpable pleasure, "neither too strong, nor too acidic." She takes the remaining half of that walnut in her hand and moves over to the dried apricots. Selecting one of her favorite varieties, the Extra Jumbo, she sandwiches the cracked walnut between the spongy fruits, colored like a deep Andean mountain sunset. The rich apricot nut flavor melts in the mouth like a sip of well-blended cognac.

"There is a lot of curative power through eating apricots, cherries, or walnuts—they are good for the body," she says with perspicacious wisdom.

During the winter season, Olson produces four sizes of dried Blenheim apricots—a Chinese variation that was brought along Western trade routes and reached California, via the missionaries, in the early eighteenth century. To dry the fruits, Olson places them on large trays under the sun where they are dried for three to five days. There, they wrinkle and bend, developing skins that appear worn like brushed hide. The interiors, however, are moist, tender, and intensely flavored.

Olson's smile does not camouflage her fear that each crop may be the last. Most of the family's remaining land is leased from the city of Sunnyvale. At any point, the city could elect to sell that land and end the Olsons' century-long legacy.

"We only continue because it's a labor of love, and we enjoy the fruits," Olson says, her father agreeing.

Local residents who can find the fruits without driving deep into the countryside may not know how lucky they are, or how quickly that luck may fade into a hazy horizon of houses.

"Don't remove the pits from the cherries when making clafoutis. The pit is what gives the good taste."

SYLVAIN PORTAY

Ripe nectarines

The academic appearance of his scattered office -- filled with books, papers, and diplomas -- belies Art Lange's trade. Although a doctor in plant physiology (the study of plant growth and reproduction), Lange no longer spends his days in University lecture halls, but walking through nectarine orchards on his Honey Crisp Farm south of Fresno, California.

The son of a dairy farmer from Washington State, Lange now specializes in growing the nectarine, a firm and fuzzless peach, simply because it is something he has always wanted to do. Recalling the impressions of his childhood, he muses, "we had our own fruit trees, that's probably when I got my first taste of good fruit, and I never could understand why I couldn't get such sweet fruit in the grocery stores."

He now knows why. Due to a short shelf life, "ripe fruit is a rare thing in our society," Lange contends. According to him, because people are not familiar with fully mature fruits, they have little idea what to do when they find them, "even if ripe fruits were on the shelves, people would squeeze them to death." He laughingly recalls a woman who, making her way through a display of his ripe nectarines, ruined every one. "When I asked what she was doing," Lange tells, "the woman responded, 'I'm trying to find a really good one.'"

By waiting until the last minute to harvest, at the peak of ripeness, Lange has been able to capture the most intense flavors of all the fruits he grows.

"I pick the fruits, on average, about one week to ten days after my neighbors pick the same variety," Lange asserts. "In other words, they are commercial growers."

While Lange markets the nectarines and other fruits he grows at the ranch, including peaches, apricots, and plums, he does so only to farmers' markets across California, through a professional distributor, or, more recently, by mail order. In light of the fruits' delicate condition, commercial handling would literally tear them apart.

A ripe fruit, although more difficult to manage, releases the richest concentration of flavor and juice. By virtue of staying on the tree longer, the fruit has had time to collect additional sugar. "That's what makes the fruit so delectable," Lange enthuses. The buyer has only to eat the fruit promptly to enjoy its best qualities.

The grower, on the other hand, has the more difficult task of deciding when the fruit is ready for harvest. To get the best specimen, "take the fruit when the base color is right and the skin has lost some of its shine and gently tug, but don't press. If it resists, it is probably not ripe," Lange instructs. "Smell it," he urges, noting that

the flavor should come through the skin. "Take a bite," he finally directs, a slight smile curving the corners of his mouth. Some of the ripest fruit may not be the most beautiful, "but man, it's so sweet," he exhales.

Lange's older trees produce 30 different varieties of nectarines. All display different textured fleshes, colors -- varying from white to yellow -- and aromas, ranging from an almost gamy intensity to ambrosia sweetness.

Out of all his fruits, Lange favors the snowqueen nectarine—a fragile, sweet fruit with a nice balance between acid and sugar. He smiles mischievously, "you really have to take a bite of it. It's the only way to know if it is truly ripe." An invitation few people refuse.

"Instead of apples, use the nectarines to make a tarte Tatin, cutting the nectarines into slices of about one-third of an inch thick."

SYLVAIN PORTAY

Ohio peaches

"Peaches from Ohio?" That's the question most people ask when told that the midwestern state yields some of America's finest fuzzy fruits.

"The best in the world," clarifies Lee Jones, a greens and vegetable farmer from the shores of Lake Erie. Jones has a unique way to describe the peaches his friend Brad Phillips harvests from a small farm in Berlin Heights, located 50 miles west of Cleveland. After a measurable pause, Jones begins to speak, gaining a rushing momentum with each word.

"It's going to be messy because when you bite that peach, it's going to be so full of juice that it's going to dribble right down your chin. And you're not going to let that get away. You're gonna get after that because it's full of sugar. It's just an amazing flavor. You have a peach in one hand and a hanky in the other."

Phillips, the latest in a long line of farmers, the first of whom settled in Ohio in 1817, assumes more humility in discussing his successful peaches. Standing under one of his trees, Phillips explains that Lake Erie, which rests just down a sloping hill, keeps the orchard from warming too early in the spring and cooling off too quickly in the fall.

"We have 200 feet of elevation in only four miles," Phillips says, pointing his finger toward the blue expanse of lake. "So the cold air tends to flow down," away from the trees.

During the glacial period, the lake covered the area that is now Berlin Heights. As the temperature rose, the water retreated and left behind a deposit of sandy soil, "almost sand dunes in some areas," says Phillips. Due to the looser soil, the ground "drains very well," allowing the trees to grow at a slower, less vigorous rate. "They spend more time putting sugar into the fruits and less energy into the wood." As a result, the fruits get sweeter at a faster rate.

Phillips can harvest his first peaches days before his neighbors who grow the fruits further inland on heavier soil. Still, Phillips is patient and waits until the last, perfect minute to handpick the fruit at its peak.

"He feels the peach. If it's not right for him today, he'll introduce himself to the peach tomorrow and, then, will harvest it at its full ripeness," says Jones, whose favorite variety of the fruit is the Red Haven.

Phillips produces 15 varieties of peaches through the growing season. The earliest ripen in July, while the last turn a velvety orange rose in September. Ranging in colors from yellow to white, they all differ in shape, peeling ease, and sweetness.

In order to maintain the high quality of his fruits, Phillips's production, routinely sold out in the local market, remains very limited. When asked if he has ever tried the rival Georgia peaches, Phillips simply replies, "Why should I? I have my own."

"Peal the peach and cut it into quarters, add a bit of honey, lemon juice and some water. Magnificent!"

JEAN-LOUIS PALLADIN

Pick up the pecan

Amid the high-rise buildings of Phoenix and low-flying planes preparing to land at the nearby airport, a field of pecan trees emerges like the proverbial oasis in a desert. Clustered inside the thick leaves of the trees, prime nuts teasingly wait to fall to the ground. One man eagerly awaits that moment.

Wayne Smith, founder of The Farm at the South Mountain, began to work with pecans almost by chance. Years ago, biking down a road lined with dozens of the trees, he noticed roadside property that was for sale. Unfortunately, the land and crops were in poor condition as the proprietor was an elderly gentleman who had not been able to work the soil for some time. Suffering from negligence, the pecan trees, which had been planted in the 1920s, were deteriorating. Upon purchasing the property, Smith immediately tended to the 100 trees, watering them religiously and pruning them with care. Today, he harvests approximately 5,000 pounds of pecans per year and grows ten different varieties of the long nut.

Sitting outside at a wooden table under a tree, Smith leans over and picks up a quarter-moon-shaped nut. Holding it in his hand, he calls it the Success Nut. He easily cracks it open and pops it in his mouth. From the bottom of a neighboring tree, he plucks a longer nut, the Western Schley, and does the same, smiling broadly through crunching noises.

Pecans, also grown and widely consumed in Georgia and Texas, come in a variety of tastes and sizes. "But you have to try them at the same time to really taste the differences," Smith claims. "Eat them with their skin," he suggests, arguing in the same breath that a diet of pecans, dates, and water alone could fully nourish a human body. With, perhaps, a touch of the incredibly rich dark pecan honey also made on the farm.

With his 100-tree orchard, Smith does not compete with growers who manage larger, 10,000-acre orchards in nearby Green Valley. During the harvesting season, which, appropriately, takes place between the nut-trimmed holidays of Thanksgiving and Christmas, people simply wander into Smith's garden and, without authority, indulge in a free-for-all picking frenzy.

Smith laughs at the clear profit loss. Apparently, this nut grower would much rather watch people enjoying in their mouth what he enjoys so much growing in his fields.

"I toss the pecans in hot oil and then sprinkle them with cumin and cayenne for a salad garnish."

HALLIE HARRON

HERBS
&
FLOWERS

The Lazy Susan Ranch

If there was to be an herb heaven, the Lazy Susan Ranch would be its divine space and Linda-Marie Loeb, its goddess.

There is little mystery as to why chefs in the San Francisco area have a certain reverence for Loeb's ranch, located in the hills overlooking Calistoga, California, in northern Napa Valley. Not only has she developed an estate where she grows a seemingly infinite variety of herbs, but she also retains a poetic knowledge of most flora.

"I love herbs for their shapes, colors, tastes, and above all, their fragrances," she muses standing along a pathway lined with lush green plants.

Her passion began long before she launched her 80-acre ranch. Years ago, Loeb owned the Moa Room, a restaurant in San Francisco. "I was growing herbs only as a hobby while I was working at other endeavors," she smiles before breaking into a solid laugh, "and it got out of control." She fondly assigns blame to her restaurant partner who wanted to cook with the herbs regularly. She expanded her then private garden to accommodate the restaurant, but "once the word spread about our herbs, we started selling to other chefs."

Determined to leave the city, Loeb searched for the ideal location in which to develop her small garden. "I wanted an old house that had not already been spoiled by someone fixing it up the wrong way, and I wanted a property that had the mature plantings that we have here."

After two years of patient search in the Napa Valley, she found the Lazy Susan Ranch, a farm built in 1879 and originally constructed to house livestock and store homegrown grapes. While the owners had used the farm to make wine during prohibition, the subsequent generation ripped out all the grapevines and planted prunes instead. Later, the farm turned to chestnut and orange crops, "it was the only farm in Napa Valley where you could see orange trees commercially grown," Loeb says pointing to a row of remaining trees. In Napa, oranges were not as profitable as grapes and the winter weather common to the entire valley area made orange growing difficult. Nonetheless, since the ranch is located above the valley, "the wind sweeps the coldest air away" and leaves behind a warm temperature ideal for growing oranges and herbs.

"I sometimes feel guilty, it is like cheating," Loeb says humbly, turning toward the nearby hills. "It is so easy for me to do what I do well just because of the natural circumstances which I have nothing to do with."

Built into an incline of white stone terraces, the herb beds are angled to allow for ample drainage. Proper drainage enables the soil to support the herbs for longer seasons and is essential for all types of thyme, thistle,

and lavender. "Any herb that grows in the Mediterranean region is used to well-drained sandy soils," Loeb explains. "But if you live in a flat place in the Napa Valley area, you receive too much water in the winter and the plants are flooded—they either die or become dormant." She readily sympathizes with her fellow herb growers located further down in the valley who, unlike her, have to contend with cooler weather, shorter seasons, and more level grounds.

The richness of the soil at the Lazy Susan Ranch also favors herb planting. Due to its high content of organic material, the soil is "vigorous," says Loeb as she gathers a fistfull of the red dirt. Rubbing her fingers together lightly, she lets it sift slowly down to the ground, "the soil is what remains of the ancient bed of the Russian River, which millions of years ago, ran straight through here." In contrast, the white and chalky soil found in southern Napa Valley is more appropriate for grape growing.

Loeb takes pride in the fact that, instead of growing grapes, she has cultivated her land for a unique, if not exotic, crop. "I think that I am making a contribution because, in the long run, growing only grapes is not really good for the water and the animal resources."

Row upon row of herbs line the groves, drawing the ranch's landscape into myriad colors, shapes, and aromas. Stepping among the plants, a wealth of new ideas for seasoning and decorative presentation come to mind.

Consider, for example, sage. Loeb grows five different varieties: garden green, Berggarten, golden, tri-color, and purple. Loeb points out their differences. The golden sage enlivens any plate with its colorful yellow stripes. And the purple sage, with its deep, velvety texture, simply "makes you want to pick and feel it," Loeb says smiling, herself unable to resist as she bends to rub a leaf. "It is quite dramatic."

Indeed, herbs are not only about flavor, but also about visual appeal. Enhancing the herbs' natural qualities can be painstaking, however. Pineapple mint, with variegated snow-white and green leaves, is a prime illustration. Although the plant bears a strong pineapple flavor, its primary virtue is the striking appearance of its white leaf. "But the white leaves are not a dominant feature, it has a tendency to revert to all green. So we are constantly out in the garden trimming the herbs so that the white part survives," Loeb explains.

Around an old fountain nestled on a hill below the house, Loeb has structured a small garden where she grows a private collection of herbs and flowers. The plants are not necessarily edible, but the palate of brilliant colors illuminates the property and some bear stories worth telling. The rue, gray green with small teardrop-shaped leaves and tiny yellow flowers, is one of those specimens. While traveling in Peru in 1998, Loeb noticed in the old town of Cisco that the door of every house and shop had a bundle of freshly cut rue sitting in a pot. "People just believe the plant wards off evil spirits," she says, narrating the tale. "I grow it myself simply because I love the story."

The stinging nettle is a relatively nondescript green weed that sprouts a white flower and is used to make a spring tonic soup in Ireland and some parts of France. Yet, the plant is virtually unknown on the West Coast of the United States. A powerful herb, it stings the skin on contact. The French singer, Serge Gainsbourg, had a particular fondness for the herb because, as he said, "it is the only herb that defends itself against humans." While the stinging nettle is not poisonous, the burn can be uncomfortable and last for several minutes, if not a full day. To heal or soothe the sting, Loeb suggests rubbing the common dock weed on the affected area.

A favorite aspect of Loeb's work is growing herbs and flowers not typically available in the area and then inviting chefs in for a sampling. She recently presented the borage, which bears a delicate, edible blue flower that is often used in decorating pastry. A versatile plant, it also produces a nutritious leaf that releases a cucumber flavor popular in traditional Italian recipes.

Chefs are more than just privy to a large choice of herbs and flowers, they also receive special attention as the products are brought, freshly cut, directly to their kitchens. Loeb has a certain harvesting practice. She cuts the herbs in the morning after the dew has begun to dry, but before the sun has warmed the air. The herbs are then chilled immediately, but not washed, because once water contacts the leaves of certain delicate herbs, such as basil, the decomposition process begins. Loeb waits until the last minute to wash the herbs, before cooking them or placing them on the plate. She stresses that the herbs should never be stored in a plastic bag, but wrapped in a damp paper towel and kept in a refrigerator.

When handled with care, herbs and flowers will last much longer, taste more flavorful, and appear beautiful when served at the table. This, Loeb ensures as Napa Valley's patroness of sweet-smelling and tender-tasting plants.

"Mix your selection of herbs with seasoned butter and stick them under the skin of poultry before cooking, or serve them on a barbecued piece of meat."

SYLVAIN PORTAY

91

Filé powder

In the deep bayou of southern Louisiana, the food is as complex and diverse as the population. And nothing displays the rich culinary heritage of its inhabitants -- Native American, French, Cajun, Creole, African, and West Indian -- as colorfully as the New Orleans farmer's market.

Also known as Crescent City Farmer's Market, it is filled throughout the year with growers, farmers, and fishermen from the local region as well as throughout the state. Located just feet away from the French Quarter, the market attracts curious visitors and *habitués*—those who, coming every Saturday, could not picture culinary life without it.

In a select corner sits one man—the picture of southern character and elegance. Lionel Key, with a straight back and warm, relaxed smile, carefully prepares the ultimate Cajun condiment: filé powder. He pounds a rounded pestle made of cypress wood into a heavy pecan-wood mortar in rhythmic motion. At the bottom of the mortar, a fine, moss-colored silken powder is made from the young, dried leaves of sassafras trees. Originally a tradition of the Choctaw Indians, the powder is used to thicken and flavor old-fashioned Creole gumbos—soup stews made of crawfish, meat, or vegetables. Although the sassafras tree, from which Key handpicks his leaves, is found along the eastern seaboard -- from Maine down to Louisiana -- the seasoning is strictly southern.

Along with the traditional, local "spice" that Key brings to the market, is the equally colorful story of his filé. Key's recipe was passed down from his blind great uncle, Uncle Bill, who for more than fifty years made the powder which was celebrated as the best in the region. Just two years before Uncle Bill died, Key, whose nickname was "Boo," asked for the secret family recipe for filé. Thrilled to pass on the legacy, Uncle Bill gave Key his mortar and pestle -- carved in 1904 by a family member -- and the formula for making the unique filé.

At the market, Key is only too pleased to demonstrate the pounding of leaves into powder, the final step in creating his product. Yet when asked, as he is by many people, about his methods for harvesting, drying, and curing the leaves, Key gently laughs. Friendly, but firm, he shakes his head slowly from left to right. He offers a sampling of his powder, but those secrets shared by Uncle Bill will remain within the family.

Key remembers what Uncle Bill often told him: "My Boo, a lot of people make filé but they don't make it like me." Today, no one makes the local spice like Boo.

Running squirrel and the wild salads

Running Squirrel has no proven scientific theory to distinguish edible flowers or plants from poisonous ones. Half Cherokee, he simply follows his family tradition of picking the best wild salads that grow in the mountains surrounding the Columbia River Gorge in Washington and Oregon States.

"My uncle taught me everything," Running Squirrel says with sober reverence when asked about his methods for harvesting wild greens. Beginning at age six, Running Squirrel, whose name was given by his mother in honor of "the squirrels that ran across the dirt floor in the cabin" (his legal name is Earl Ahern), spent most of his youth scouring southwestern Oregon's narrow mountain passages and roadsides for succulent leaves. Now, more than fifty years later, his handpicked greens are served at the finest restaurants from New York to Los Angeles.

Wild salads and flowers have a richer, less bitter flavor than most salad leaves and are particularly aromatic. Despite their colorful characteristics, the plants are elusive in the rugged mountains and can be found only in certain contained spots. "People think they know the plant because they saw a picture of it," Running Squirrel says skeptically while driving his old, white truck along the gorge in search of lemon balm and miner's lettuces. "To find the plants, they have to know the habitat and how to bring them back home."

He pulls off the road and, wandering into the forest underbrush, finds a cluster of lemon balm—a dark green leaf bearing a lemony aroma nearly as potent as a spray of perfume. Close by, under the long oak tree shadows, he finds the miner's lettuce. A common Native American food, the plant bears small, round leaves and white blossoms, and yields a slightly sweet flavor. Running Squirrel's fingers move nimbly through the extraordinarily moist dirt and settle on the wood violet, a flower with such high levels of vitamin C that one blossom can fulfill the daily dietary requirement.

"Time is our worst enemy," Running Squirrel announces softly, standing up with a straight back. Explaining that the plants must constantly be kept moist, he dips his collected cluster into the fresh springwater of nearby creeks and prepares to rapidly transport them home. On the way to his truck, he points to a striking and brilliant blue-flowered plant. "It's poisonous," Running Squirrel says, before adding, "most likely deadly." Following the inexhaustible man, there hardly seems to be a seed in the forest that he can't identify on sight.

Running Squirrel began selling his salads when, after years of foraging, he recognized that his products were viable haute cuisine. He had heard of Charles Novy, the founder of Fresh and Wild, a wild mushroom distributor for restaurants across the United States, and decided to introduce himself.

Novy recalls their first encounter with an amused, gentle smile. "I said, 'why do you think you can do this job? How do you know that what you are selling me isn't poisonous?'" Novy recalls that Running Squirrel responded with confidence, explaining that throughout his childhood he had worked with, and eaten as part of his regular diet, all the plants he planned to offer. Novy pressed on, challenging the man.

"I asked him if he had any literature that I could look at, and he did—a very good book on wild herbs." Novy concludes the story with undisguised admiration. "Running Squirrel opened the book and looked up various plants, reciting their scientific names. He had taught himself all the science on his own!" The two men began their collaboration soon thereafter.

Running Squirrel spends three-quarters of every day in the dense forests searching for hundreds of varieties of greens and flowers. "It's not work to me. I enjoy it," Running Squirrel says in a relaxed voice. He enjoys it so much that he moved from Washougal, a small, but active town near the Columbia River, to an isolated house tucked in a thicket 15 miles away.

The wet weather and the dramatic, profoundly moist terrain of the mountains, featured in Stanley Kubrick's movie *The Shining*, favor rich vegetation. Since the 1980 volcanic eruption of Mount St. Helens in Washington, plants and flowers are even more abundant. Running Squirrel finds some of the best plants at 2,000 feet, where the colder habitat -- 15° lower than in the nearby valley -- produces a slower growth rate. "Higher plants are stronger, juicer," Running Squirrel explains. A high-altitude plant found in the damp ground of thick woods called the Alaska ginseng, or the devil's club, is a paradoxical growth. While the plant's spines can cause infections, the the root's bark is used in teas for healing purposes. "It's the best thing I have ever found," Running Squirrel says excitedly. "Thanks to it, my kids have more gumption and energy."

Not far from the trail of Lewis and Clark, watercress can be found in small streams running beside the road. "If you cut them too close to the bottom," he warns, "then they will turn yellow." Along the same isolated road, Running Squirrel digs deep into the dirt to extract the chemist plant. "The Indians survived on it," he explains. "The bitter, but nourishing flower is edible, and the root -- white and sweet -- is used to bake tacos or burritos." Finally, he pulls out a wood sorrel which, with heart-shaped cloverlike leaves, bears a crunchy, green apple flavor. "My mother mixed it with bumblebee honey to top biscuits and cookies," Running Squirrel shares somewhat shyly.

Along with salads, Running Squirrel harvests flowers in the Washington and Oregon mountains. His collection includes yellow mustard, which belongs to the broccoli family and has a peppery flavor, the wild lily, which produces tender, purple leaves, and, Running Squirrel's preference, the wild rose. He claims that the soft, flavorful petals of the wild rose are "excellent in salads."

Accompanied by his dog, Running Squirrel lives his days in the high mountains. Nothing pleases him more than exploring the thousands of acres of jagged trails and worn valleys, which he knows by heart, for the elusive emerald greens. Nothing, except, the companionship of his two sons who also wish to carry on the Cherokee tradition of finding America's wildest salads and flowers, as taught only by Running Squirrel.

"For wild salads, it's very simple: Add a lime vinaigrette."

JEAN-LOUIS PALLADIN

MEAT

Makache, cattle from Arizona

More than a century ago, the last Apache battled against one-third of the American army in the mountains of Arizona and New Mexico. When Geronimo, their leader, was captured in 1886, he recognized that his fight against the white settlers was futile. An era had come to an end.

Once great warriors, many of the Apache have become cowboys, raising and breeding cattle on their reservation northeast of San Carlos, Arizona. Today, a group of Apache cowboys work hand in hand with Will Holder—an American cowboy who combines traditional cattle ranching methods with an unusual respect for animals and their environment. The all natural, grass-fed beef Holder produces reflects the flavors and scents of Arizona's wild, open lands.

Beside a stretch of seemingly endless road that crosses the Apache reservation, accessible only with special permit, Apache cowboys tag a herd of newborn calves. Holder watches closely, standing beside Apache, Alvin Nosie. In nine months, Holder will purchase his calves from this same Apache herd. As Holder looks on, Nosie slowly moves his gaze from the young calves to the wide sweep of the 88,000-acre Apache ranch. Roaming on the expansive high plain surrounded by arid mountains, the scattered 1,000 cows and calves appear like small black dots against the horizon. With approximately 65,000 total cattle on the reservation, Nosie constantly rotates his herd of cows from one pasture to another in order to preserve the grass.

"One cowboy can run up 200 heads of *makache* -- the Apache word for cow -- and drive them by himself," Nosie proudly points out.

Not far away, beyond the cliffs, Holder also moves his herd to new pastures, riding his horse for hours every day to do so. Convinced that healthy animals and good beef require a balanced environment, he and his wife, Jan, not only avoid overgrazing the land but have gone one step further to back the reintroduction of the Mexican gray wolf to the area.

"We need to learn how to work with and not against nature," asserts Jan.

"The better my environment, the better my beef," Holder echoes. "It's not an either-or proposition."

Bearing this philosophy, in the early 1990s, the Holders decided to leave behind their advertising careers in Phoenix and move to the Anchor Ranch, near the New Mexico border, where Holder was born. Today, as the fourth generation of ranchers in the remote Blue Mountain region, two and one-half hours away from the nearest Wal-Mart, the Holders try to keep the cowboy tradition alive while restoring the cattle rancher's embattled reputation.

"There has been a lot of damage done to the public land in the past two hundred years, but it is not the cattle that are the problem, it's the people," says Jan.

The historical difficulty with cattle ranching has been its impact on the land. For centuries, the routine practice of ranchers involved leaving cattle unattended in the mountains for long periods of time. Sharing space with elk and deer, the livestock overgrazed the fertile strips of land, causing significant ecological damage.

Holder's ranching methods avoid such complications. Waking every morning before dawn, he mounts his horse and moves 100 Hereford and Black Angus cattle around the 10,000 acres of land he leases from the government. Beginning at 5,000 feet above sea level, in a dried river valley called Eagle Creek, Holder's property rises up to a high of 7,500 feet. With the help of a map, he studies the region's vegetation and the living habits of the intermixing animal life. Careful not to disturb the natural balance of the surroundings, including the natural grass growth, he decides where to direct his cattle.

Holder keeps in mind the several natural predators that inhabit the arid mountains, including bears, mountain lions, bobcats, and coyotes. When the Holders supported the reintroduction of the wolves to the mountains in 1998, they surprised and angered many of their neighbors, including the Apache. Their decision had not been anticipated, in part, because Holder's grandfather, Eugene Cleveland, had allegedly killed the last free-roaming wolf in the region nearly fifty years prior.

The fears surrounding wolves, however, appear ill founded. Since 1998, the Holders have not lost one head of cattle. Ironically, prior to the animal's comeback, Will lost an average of eight heads per year to predators.

"We're trying to train the wolves not to eat the cattle, but the rabbits and the deer," Holder explains. The herd's nearly daily rotation makes it difficult for the wolf to track. Instead, the wolves stalk the prolific population of elk and deer which, although appealing, tend to "sit down on the 'ice-cream' part of the pasture," as Jan says, until there is nothing left but dirt. Thus, the wolf's presence actually helps preserve a natural balance.

Despite the outcry from several ranchers, Holder is serious about his position and defends it steadfastly.

"If you can construct an environment that maximizes the diversity of the landscapes and animals, then you will be able, in essence, to produce more grass, animals, plants, and birds," he argues. "But if you take a wolf out of the environment, other things are going to go, too."

Riding his horse, which he personally trained, Holder embodies the cowboy tradition. He wears a large black hat to protect him from the sun, brown leather chaps, which preserve his jeans and ease saddle riding, and a silk scarf around his neck to block the cool morning air or afternoon heat. Two border collies, who answer to Mycroft and Maggie, are Holder's only company.

"The whole way of life just seems to have gone away," Jan observes wistfully, noting that trucks and helicopters have long since replaced horses on several ranches.

Riding slowly up the slippery hills, Holder is gentle with the rust- and cream-colored calves. "I never yell at the cattle because it stirs them up." Only a few words he directs at the dogs, or an occasional bark from Maggie when an animal strays, interrupt the windy quiet of the hills.

Holder's method of work is unusual. Many cowboys, playing with ropes and charging the horses, collect the cattle with demonstrative force. Instead, Holder moves his horse slowly into "the flight zone," the animal's area of private space which, if disturbed, will cause the animal to flee. At any given point in moving the cattle, Holder remains on the fringe of the flight zone. He has only to move slightly in the direction he wishes the cattle to move to get a seemingly magical response from the herd.

"When people see it happen, they are shocked to the point of disbelief that it can work that way. They think that I tricked them or something devious is at work here," Holder says, laughing. Arriving on a narrow trail down a steep slope, the cattle step in line without panicking as Holder follows closely behind.

Upon reaching their final destination, the animals begin grazing the pasture, golden under the sun's reflection. Due in large part to Holder's effort to protect the flora, food is abundant. Rabbit brush, juniper, and pinion trees add to blue and black gramma, curly mesquite, and cactus. The crops renew at a faster rate because they have never been worn to the ground. After the "fabulous, violent thunderstorms of July and August that just dump inches of rain down in hours, all this turns green instantly," says Jan, adding that September is the most beautiful month of the year.

Not only are the cattle able to select the grass that they eat, but their diet is free of foreign, manmade substances. By at the age of sixteen to eighteen months, the marbling, or inner muscular fat, has formed and the steer are ready for slaughter. While cattle raised in barns on a fixed grain diet mature twice as quickly, the feed is often hormone laden.

Confronting criticism that, because his animals exercise daily, the final beef may be tough, wild tasting, and not as consistent as grain-fed cattle, Holder couldn't be more unequivocal. He asserts that the young age of the animal and the stress-free environment in which it has been raised yield a tender, juicier beef that bears the subtle flavors of the vegetation. Regarding questions of consistency, he sees a lack of uniformity as a quality—each steer reflects its own history and diet and provides an unique flavor.

Holder traces the beef's superior character to its Apache-bred origin. The Apache line of Hereford "is so old that it's one of those very good lines, tender and flavorful," he says. In fact, the Apache, who began raising cattle in the 1930s, agreed to sell their animals to Holder because they had the assurance that he was using neither antibiotics nor hormones with his animals. In a pleased manner, they observed him apply the Apache philosophy in raising makache: "work 'em, work 'em, work the cattle."

The work starts when Holder takes over the weaned calves from their mothers. While he could truck the animals to his property, he prefers to use an old American tradition, the cattle drive. On his horse, and over the course of four days, he slowly herds his calves from the Apache plains to his ranch beyond the mountains. Although less expensive, Will uses this method because little stress is involved for the animal.

Whether riding his horse or driving his truck, Will Holder (right, with a calf) has every reason to be pleased with the beef he produces. His calves come from the San Carlos Apache tribe, where he has established a good work relationship. Every year, Alvin Nosie (bottom left) provides Holder with calves ready for a cattle drive. Holder's animals then freely roam on the 10,000 acres of open land. By moving them everyday, he prevents the cattle from overgrazing and ensures their safety against the Mexican Gray Wolves.

"If you drive them on horseback, and do it gently and take your time, not only do they learn to herd right away, but they also seem to take comfort in moving along," claims Jan.

An important advantage with the cattle drive, which the Apache celebrate with dance and music, is that the animals don't get sick. "If you walk them in a stress-free way, I have zero sick loss. When I tell ranchers that, they don't believe me, they think that I am lying or bragging. But I'm not," Holder asserts.

Working to minimize the stress levels includes efforts made right before slaughter. Holder takes the time to gently load each steer onto the trailer as it leaves the ranch. He also avoids modern slaughter houses where animals are often killed too quickly, often at a rate of 2,000 per day. Instead, Holder uses the services of the University of Arizona in Tucson, six hours away, where only six cattle are slaughtered per day. Still, he hopes to build his own facility in the future where he can assume control of all the beef production.

Despite the unique qualities of the Holderses' beef and their dedication to protect the environment and its inhabitants, certain environmentalist groups still lobby against the cattle ranchers in Arizona. The Holders argue, with wounded and bewildered emotion, that such efforts, if successful, would effectively end the cowboy tradition and the recently developed economic ties between native and nonnative Americans.

"We've become more of a community. Our economics sort of depend on one another," says Holder. "The white man has done nothing good for the Apache and they harbor a lot of resentment for good reason. It's only because my family has been in this area for so long that we've built up a relationship with the tribe."

The Holders are not the only people to value cattle ranching. According to Nosie, cattle ranching impacts the lives of 8,000 of the 12,000 San Carlos Apache tribe.

Still, when asked who he considers the Apache hero today, the Apache cowboy or Geronimo, Nosie replies, "Geronimo, still." After a short silence, he adds, "mean, but a hero."

Holder reflects on the meaning of being a cowboy and looks off somewhere into the huge land. "A love of the open West, of open spaces, of the desert, the sunsets, the stark beauty of the place."

Sharing one thing in common, both men want to pass on to their sons what they take so much pride in being, an American cowboy.

"To make the most flavorful preparations, marinate a skirt steak with a lot of fresh garlic, olive oil, and fresh chiles. Then rub the meat with sel de Guérande, and grill it over mesquite wood. Serve it rare, of course!"

ALESSANDRO STRATTA

White and pink veal

In the rolling hills of Virginia, once the stage of violent Civil War battles, calves roam freely with mother cows, intermittently nursing and grazing on fields of grass. Instead of the more common white European-style veal, these calves will develop a rose-colored meat.

White and pink veal both are derived from calves of related breeds, but calves raised in quite different manners. The resulting flavors are distinct—the pink veal, or baby beef, bears a complex, strong flavor while white veal meat is sweet and mild.

"If the calf is not allowed to live and forage outside, then the meat is similar to the white veal," explains Jamie Nicoll, who farms calves with pink meat in southern Virginia. Raised free-range and able to exercise, the animal develops a meat enriching hemoglobin which causes the rose-colored hue to the flesh. In contrast, white veal calves enjoy a milk-based diet and are raised indoors in a more controlled environment. That way, "we can monitor the health and the well-being of the animal," says Stephen Pryzant, a white-veal farmer based in northeastern Pennsylvania.

Born in Charlottesville, Virginia, the historic hometown of Thomas Jefferson, Nicoll recounts that after leaving a life on Wall Street at age twenty-seven, he taught himself how to produce veal. With notepads and pencils in hand, he and his wife, Rachel, visited nearby farmers to learn exactly what to do. "I didn't even know that a cow had four teats," he confesses. He purchased a pregnant cow and named it Pava, the Russian word for cow. Bringing home his "big white animal with a few black spots," he gave milking his first try.

"She kicked the hell out of my knee," he says, remembering the pain that kept him in bed for two days.

Nicoll quickly learned that Pava was producing 100 pounds of milk a day, far more than her anticipated offspring would require. Trying to dispose of the excess milk, Nicoll first sold it to his mother's friends. But then he began to play with the idea of using the milk to raise extra calves; calves, however, that he had yet to acquire. Thus, with only one cow, one calf on the way, and no money in his pocket, he used his Wall-Street savvy to sell the upcoming herd of calves "on futures." As Nicoll recalls, "I knocked on doors and said, 'I'll bring you veal in eight weeks, but you have to give me the money now.'"

With his first few calves, Nicoll collected the cow's milk in a bucket and hand-fed the animals. As his herd expanded, mother cows and calves, he realized that he could simply let Mother Nature do her work. Today, his Black Angus, Charolais, and Hereford cows nurse their offspring naturally while freely grazing on the green pastures. "I just have to watch and enjoy," Nicoll says in relaxed tone.

The taste of veal varies according to the techniques employed in raising the animal, either hand-feeding (left) or allowing the calves to roam freely (right). The meat, white and sweet in the first instance, is pink and strong when the calf is raised on grass. Careful attention is given to the calves through both methods, ensuring the animals grow in a stress-free environment.

The more traditional method of hand-feeding the calves is no less rewarding. In his Pennsylvania barn, Pryzant houses 70 calves, each of which is seven to twelve days old. In contrast to Nicoll, who raises both males and females, Pryzant works exclusively with the Holstein dairy cow's male offspring.

In the barn, the calm animals play with Pryzant as he approaches. They are about to receive their morning meal of warm powdered milk. Since the calves do not venture outdoors, the barns become their familiar territory. The set meal hours of 6:00 A.M. and 6:00 P.M., the order in which they are fed, and the daily presence of Pryzant and his wife, Sylvia, make life a comfortable routine for the animals.

When the calves are four and a-half months old, Pryzant prepares them for departure. Providing a vitamin and calming sugar for the ride, he slowly loads the animals onto the truck. From there, "a local farmer takes care of them for me," Pryzant says. "He stops on the way to check on the animal." Sylvia points out that their daily efforts to maintain a stress-free life for the calves would be futile if the animal was left to become anxious at the last moment.

Separation must also be well managed on the Nicolls' farm. "Weaning is very stressful for both the mother and the calf," Nicoll says. "You have to do anything you can to lessen that." Also sent away at four and a-half months, the young herd of calves is placed in a special pasture one day before slaughter. There, Nicoll offers fresh water, grass, and hay.

The environment and the level of care provided during the sensitive first four months of a calf's life determine whether the meat, pink or white, will be a superior veal. Both Nicoll and Pryzant have perfected discrete methods for raising the animals that ensure different yet equally succulent fare.

"I like the loin of the veal the way my mother prepares it - with quarters of potatoes, pieces of carrot, and a cluster of sage. Everything is cooked in the oven and constantly basked with the cooking juices."

SANDRO GAMBA

The exotic indigenous bison

The North American bison is again roaming the United States and Canada. Once the core of Native American life, the imposing animal was nearly exterminated by American pioneers toward the end of the nineteenth century. Massive and magnificent, the bison, a distant cousin of European cattle, bears a unique low-fat, high-protein, deeply toned, and almost purplish-colored meat. Edgar Bronfman, Sr., Chairman of the Board of Joseph E. Seagram & Sons, was searching for those very qualities when he began to raise bison on his Georgetown Farm in Virginia.

"I was looking for low-cholesterol meat and tasted bison . . . I thought it was delicious," says Bronfman who first tried bison at a restaurant in Sun Valley, Idaho. He describes bison as somewhat comparable to beef, but "a touch sweeter, and because it has so little fat, it is not at all greasy or fatty to the taste." A bison convert, Bronfman will only eat beef when bison is not available, "it doesn't make you feel stuffed the way beef can."

On his 12,000-acre ranch at the foot of Virginia's Blue Ridge Mountains, approximately 5,000 animals freely roam luxuriant pastures. Among them, Thunderheart, a ten-year-old, 2,800-pound bull, assures the perpetuation of the farm's breed line. Standing seven and a half feet tall, with an ability to rotate on four feet (as opposed to two for cattle), to attain speeds of 30 miles per hour, and to display an aggressive temperament, Thunderheart, as his name suggests, strikes fear in the bravest rancher's heart. The animals are not simple to herd.

"Bison are protective of their offspring," explains Billy Salmon, sales manager at the Georgetown Farm. "They bed down in a tight fashion, protecting the young in a wagon-wheel position." Extremely independent, a calf is able to get on its feet and roam with the herd within forty-eight hours of birth. Although a member of the bovine family, bison remain wild animals.

According to the National Bison Association, at the end of the Ice Age the estimated bison population in North America, the animal's sole habitat, ranged between 30 and 70 million. The arrival of white settlers in America marked not only the introduction of domesticated cattle but also the decimation of bison.

"A theory says that by eliminating the bison, settlers hoped to eliminate the Native Americans," Salmon says. American Indians maintained a religious reverence for the animal and utilized nearly every part of the bison, or *tatonka,* as a staple of their culture. "Native Americans actually moved their homes and villages as the bison moved up and down the continent," Salmon explains. "It was their diet, their shelter, their

Bison was nearly extinct two centuries ago. This member of the bovine family is indigenous to North America and once roamed widely throughout the continent. Because its meat and hide were central to the American Indian's diet and culture, newly arrived settlers nearly eradicated the species in warfare against the Native Americans. The small bison population that survived was eventually protected by the U.S. government. Its comeback as a gourmet food ensures consistent growth in the number of bison and also enforces its identity as the quintessential American food.

clothes." Although the meat served as the main resource, the skin, bones, skull, and horns were also used to make arrow points, moccasins, teepees, and blankets.

However, by the mid- to late 1800s, between the life-sustaining hunts of the Native Americans and the random slaughters executed by white Americans, the bison population was reduced to a mere 600 head.

Recognized as an endangered species in the early 1900s, herds slowly began to recover. Today, approximately 350,000 bison populate North America including the 110,000 animals located in Canada. The reintroduction of bison as a gourmet food product has inspired public interest not only in the animal's succulent steaks, but in its place in American culture.

Historically referred to as buffalo, which, according to Salmon was a name derived from "French explorers who, intrigued when they saw herds moving like a black mass, related them to the water buffalo," the animal has since reclaimed its original and proper name.

On Georgetown Farm, bison graze naturally, free from hormones, steroids, stimulants, and antibiotics. The animals are only handled by people ninety days preceding slaughter, when they are fed a special diet of grain used to ensure the meat's tenderness and consistency. Since bison meat is naturally lean and does not develop marbling or fat, the animals are harvested upon reaching a weight of 1,200 pounds, usually between the ages of twenty-four and twenty-eight months. This specific weight ensures a consistent size of primals— steaks, roasts, and other cuts.

Much in the manner of the Native American tradition, Salmon makes use of all the animal's products, including the skin and horns. Every fall, Native American tribes gather at Georgetown Farm to dance and sing in celebration of the bison.

Salmon admits that much remains to be learned about the Native American practice of handling the bold and wild bison. He smiles broadly, eager to learn those secrets that would further assist him in producing the ultimate American red meat from the legendary American animal.

"Sear the bison tenderloin in a sauté (frying) pan coated in olive oil for three to four minutes on each side, and serve it immediately. Accompany it with a flat cake of zucchini and tomatoes, truffle oil, and parmesan, but no butter."

ALAIN LECOMTE

Pigs raised on apples

The 32 English Berkshire piglets never fail to greet Stephen and Sylvia Pryzant with games as they enter the barn. Nibbling and biting the couple's heels and shoelaces, they anxiously await their daily treat, juicy apples.

In 1998, the Pryzants followed the advice of their New York friend, chef Wayne Nish, to raise apple-fed pigs. Since then, while providing an uniquely succulent meat, the playful animals have kept the American-Tunisian couple entertained at their farm in Honesdale, Pennsylvania.

"They're wonderful, they love and trust you, they know that you're not going to harm them," says Sylvia who raises her animals throughout their life with visible tenderness. She loves her animals with black curly hair and quizzical looks. Far from the proverbial pigs in mud, the piglets keep astoundingly clean quarters. In one corner of the barn they have a small, unspoiled sleeping area, in another section they feed neatly, and in the far corner they maintain a discreet bathroom space. The rest of the barn is a playground where the piglets romp around a central water fountain.

Although the animals are fed from a trough in the "dining section," Sylvia often hand-feeds them apples. She has discovered that pigs can be finicky. If an apple offered is not the ideal fruit, the piglet will simply turn up its snout. "Go take your apple in the house and make applesauce or apple pie, but don't give it to me," Sylvia imagines them saying. The animals' preferred fruit is the McIntosh, a round, sweet variety that the Pryzants harvest from a nearby orchard. Spoiled, the pigs also "indulge" Rome, Mutsu, and Golden Delicious apples on occasion.

The pulpy diet, mixed with corn feed, gives the pigs' meat a richly intricate marbling—darker and fattier than that of many larger pigs. The resulting flavor is sweet, with a slight fruity bearing. The roasted meat tastes almost as though caramelized and resembles an old-fashioned candied roast.

Born on a farm in the southern tip of Pennsylvania, the piglets are nurtured on pig's milk and grain for the first six weeks. Once weaned, the baby pigs are brought to the Pryzants' estate where they spend the next six weeks subsisting on an apple-based diet. Each animal will consume 50 pounds of the fruit and attain a weight of approximately 60-65 pounds.

Raising pigs came naturally for the Pryzants, who began their farming business producing veal in 1992 and poultry in 1997. They eventually diversified their livestock in order to hasten production rotations—while a calf takes fifteen weeks to mature and a chicken ten weeks, a pig needs only six weeks of an apple diet to reach maturity.

The Pryzants met in 1975 in Israel. Sylvia was studying in Tel Aviv, while Stephen had already begun his farming career at a kibbutz. Upon returning to the United States, they had difficulty finding a bank to fund their proposed farm project. When they finally received financial backing, a violent snow storm, "the worst in the century," destroyed the roof of their barn. While only one of 98 calves was wounded, the Pryzants' production was delayed for two years. Today, they have recovered and their farm operates at full force, producing an array of tender young meats.

Although the couple specializes in immature animals for their exclusive chef clientele, the Pryzants admit that they get attached to the piglets and their quirky behavior. Both Sylvia and Stephen feel melancholy when the animals leave the farm.

Yet, a message left by a client in New York provided some heartening feedback. The man exalted that the taste of the apple-raised meat "exploded in his mouth." Whether the meat's fruity base or rich texture prompted the client's reaction, the Pryzants are only too happy to wonder as they sort through their bushels of freshly picked apples.

"Grill the pig on a wood-fire."

JEAN-LOUIS PALLADIN

119

Lambs: that will do

"Call," a Border collie trained in animal herding, runs around the heels of bleating sheep and lambs. "Come by!" shouts his owner, John Jamison, and the dog quickly lies down as silent as the stilled herd. The dog stares at the flock without blinking. Within seconds, the woolly creatures miraculously move toward Jamison. "That will do, now" says the farmer, and the dog returns to the man's side.

"These dogs like to work," boasts Jamison, who started raising lambs after leaving a career in the coal business. "They're so intense."

Four dogs help Jamison herd 200 lambs on his ranch in the Pennsylvania hills located one hour from Pittsburgh. He raises only English Dorset lambs, a variety that "breeds out of season," Jamison explains. "So we have young lambs all year round."

In California, rancher Bruce Campbell raises the English Dorset as well. He prefers the breed because, in his opinion, "it is plump from a very young age, and the meat is particularly tender."

Whether in Pennsylvania or Sonoma Valley, the lambs of these two farmers live in wide expanses of meadow where they are free to kick up their heels and feast on rich grass. Yet the regional differences produce animals with distinct flavors, each reminiscent of the individual growing environment.

"In the spring we get garlic and onion, then we get carrots, wildflowers and herbs," Jamison says of his countryside. Therefore, he asserts that during the vernal season, adding garlic to his lamb before cooking would be a gratuitous effort—it's already there.

On the other side of the country, Campbell's sheep graze on salubrious grass under oak trees. The son of a veterinarian, he was only ten years old when his passion began. "My sister and I were participating in 4H, a youth group," Campbell remembers. "We raised a baby lamb and took it to the California State Fair. Some very nice people bought the lamb at twice its valued price. So we used the money to buy two more the following year."

By the age of twenty, Campbell's childhood hobby had developed into a small but real business. Two hundred lambs were at pasture, $20,000 rested in the bank and, with ten years of experience, Campbell was already an expert on raising the woolen stock.

Today, with a relaxed smile stretching across his sunburnt face, Campbell stands on a bluff overlooking his 1,000-acre ranch. Countless sheep and lamb spot the landscape like small puffs of cumulus clouds. He swings his arm in a wide arc across the view. "I raise about 8,000 lambs per year," Campbell estimates.

Jamison's debut as a rancher was more of a coincidence. "We started the business just to stay alive." With two farms and two mortgages on his hands when he left the coal business, he chose farming as his new livelihood. "We thought that the lamb we had was better than the one in the stores," he says simply. He quickly learned that the secret of marketing good lamb was to raise a happy one.

Indeed, the environment is crucial in enhancing the quality of lamb's meat. To keep the animal healthy, with optimal proportions of fat and tender muscle, a lamb's life should be stress-free. Space is vital. Jamison rotates his lambs between pastures on his 210-acre ranch for exercise and to ensure available grass. Campbell allows for "no more than 40 heads per acre" on his ranch. The lambs are then at liberty to move about freely with little contest for the finest food.

While Jamison likes to see his sheep achieve celebrity status -- they were used in the movie *Silence of the Lambs* starring Jodie Foster -- Campbell has found a way to communicate with the animals. He unexpectedly releases small staccato bleats from his lungs. "Yes, I know how to talk to them," he admits, smiling and proud.

"To make it more tender and flavorful, let the piece of lamb age for a few days in the refrigerator before preparing. Always keep a thin layer of fat on the meat when roasting it."

SYLVAIN PORTAY

A wild game

The Axis deer stands in regal pose at the edge of a grove, its large eyes fixed hypnotically on a truck 80 feet away. In a blinding leap of antlers and speckled auburn hide, it disappears among a cluster of green trees. Undaunted, the truck continues to drive through heavy grass, rock, and dirt. On the left, a herd of Black-buck antelope, native to India, briefly appears before galloping away into the surrounding brush. Again the truck follows, tenaciously tracking the lissome animals, and disappears from sight.

For over half a century, the central region of Texas, north of San Antonio, has been a sanctuary for exotic deer and antelope. Herds of the graceful roe, including the Axis, Sika and Fallow deer, and the Blackbuck antelope, populate the fields of neighboring ranches. Brought from India and Asia in the 1940s and 50s by wealthy landowners, the animals were originally introduced to add exotic luster to the region's wildlife. Although eventually hunted as trophies, the free-ranging animals thrived and numbers soared to the point that ranchers became concerned about the animals' ability to sustain themselves. Mike Hughes, a retired engineer from Houston, watched the animals from his new house and shared the ranchers' concern. An idea grew in his mind.

Mike Hughes's interest in wild game first blossomed in Europe, where he had lived for two years. Having observed the European gusto for venison, he knew that the meat "was considered somewhat differently there than it was in the United States." He was intrigued with the harvesting techniques employed overseas and began to conceptualize ways in which the product could be harvested and marketed successfully at home. Despite his interest, he was consumed with his engineering business at the time and gave up his notion of revolutionizing venison harvesting techniques in America.

By the age of forty-three, however, Hughes was tired of heading Oceaneering International, the diving and engineering company he had launched twenty years earlier. With more than 40 offices worldwide, Hughes was "dealing more with lawyers and stockbrokers than actually doing the engineering that he loved," his wife, Elisabeth, explains. He decided to spend more time with his family and bought a ranch in Ingram, a small village on Indian Creek. Naming it the "Broken Arrow Ranch," Hughes was amazed at the wildlife that populated his 700-acre estate.

Today, Hughes harvests deer and antelope from 200 nearby ranches when surplus populations begin to amass and markets the meat to top restaurants across the country.

For over half a century, the central region of Texas has been a sanctuary for exotic deer and antelope. Herds of the graceful roe, including the Axis, Sika, and Fallow deer, and the Blackbuck antelope, populate the fields of neighboring ranches. Brought from India and Asia in the 1940s and '50s by wealthy landowners, the animals were originally introduced to add exotic luster to the region's wildlife. Although eventually hunted as trophy game, the free-ranging animals thrived, and numbers soared to the point where ranchers became concerned about the animals' ability to sustain themselves.

"I feel very fortunate to have actually had two complete lives in just one lifetime," he says in a gravelly voice, tinged with a southwestern drawl.

Yet, this success was not accomplished without hard work. Although Hughes found little challenge in convincing ranchers to embrace his idea of harvesting overpopulated ranches, persuading chefs to purchase the meat proved slightly more complex. After harvesting his first deer from the central Texas region in the mid-1970s, Hughes wasted little time and hopped on a plane bound for New York. With an Axis deer leg in an ice chest, he began his rounds of top restaurants such as Lutece and the 21 Club.

As Hughes narrates the story, upon entering Lutece, he was escorted to the kitchen where the French chef was busy closely inspecting a crate of mushrooms. The chef sent the mushrooms away, along with the man who had brought them, and turned to Hughes, "Yes, what do you have?"

"Well, what I've got here is an Axis deer leg," Hughes answered. He lay the cut of meat on the counter, remarkable for its extraordinarily thick muscle, and faced the chef.

"But, this is not a deer leg," the chef cried.

When Hughes responded that it was, the chef barked back, "what kind of deer is this?" Hughes recalls that he patiently detailed the Indian origin of the deer, as well as his harvesting practices in Texas. Smiling impishly, he continues the tale.

"So this chef pokes on it and feels the meat and says, 'How much?' When I tell him the price . . ." Feigning a heavy French accent, Hughes imitates the chef, "Ohhh, it eeezz against naturrre!!" Hughes's heavy laugh fills the porch for minutes. "I don't know how much I charged, but it was about double what he had been paying."

Hughes says he packed up his venison thinking "a disaster" had just befallen him. As he walked out the door, however, the chef suddenly yelled out, "Wait! Wait! I'll take it."

Beyond the obvious need to sell the meat to fine restaurants, Hughes was more concerned with the need to overcome what he perceived as American reluctance to consume venison.

"Only local people thought of venison as good to eat, and not *all* of the local people thought of it as good to eat," Hughes says. "The rest of the people in the United States were not even aware that these animals existed."

Inspired by the enthusiastic European taste for wild meat, Hughes was certain that he could use his engineering imagination to create a way to properly harvest the animals at home and entice an American audience. He devised a plan involving two stages which he still practices today. First, the animal is killed with one clean shot from a gun equipped with a silencer. Second, the animal is skinned, eviscerated, and refrigerated immediately on the ranch.

To accomplish the second task, Hughes designed a mobile slaughtering unit which contains the "strictest sanitary environment." This unit follows the hunter, Rick Lee, and processes the animal as soon as it is killed. Lee, who has always hunted as a hobby, is the harvest manager of Broken Arrow Ranch. He is on the road at least half of every week, driving to ranches within a 150-mile radius of Ingram. He hunts only at the rancher's request and is accompanied by a skinner and a food inspector. On his truck, with a 38-caliber rifle and 20-inch silencer in hand, Lee knows exactly the animals he wants. "We shoot them from the vehicle from a 20- to 200-yard distance," he explains, adding that only one shot, aimed directly at the head, is fired. Because a silencer is used and the gun is fired from a long distance, the deer has no time to panic. Hughes interjects, "we kill the animal on the spot, in its native habitat, with no stress." Not only is this preferable for the animal, but the meat retains its natural tenderness and flavor.

Once killed, the animal is skinned within five minutes. It is then transported back to Ingram where the entire carcas dry-ages for two days. "During this time, the muscles are relaxing," Hughes explains. The meat is then cut and aged again for two to three weeks.

Hughes believes that the Blackbuck antelope is the most difficult to pursue of all the wildlife in the region.

"These guys are really hard to harvest because the Blackbuck evolved on open land." Hughes points to one of the animals standing under the shade of a juniper tree. "Their protective instincts are to distance themselves from the threat." Comparatively, he says, deer rely on a different tactic of hiding. "They'll go off to the edge of the trees and stop, so you can drive right up and shoot them—they're thinking they are protected when they're not." The Blackbuck never afford hunters the opportunity to get that close.

"It's very frustrating," Hughes sighs, "because we have a lot of ranchers who call and say, 'we have a large surplus of Blackbuck antelope, if you'd just come and take them, we'll let you have them free.' And we just can't harvest many of them at one time." Although Hughes is careful to always pay the rancher, harvesting more than two of the elusive antelope is simply unrealistic. "The first Blackbuck is very easy to get because they all stand around and just stare at you. The second one is much more difficult . . . after that, forget it."

The central Texas climate and vegetation fit the needs of the exotic, as well as native, deer and antelope. "These animals are out here eating very natural vegetation and, as a result, they get a wide variety of plants in their diet throughout the year," Hughes explains. Accustomed to a six-month period of tropical monsoon followed by a six-month drought in Asia, the animals have acclimated perfectly to Texas's simpler environment.

"Antelope and deer will basically subsist on whatever is available at the time," says Hughes. "If the grass is gone, they'll eat forbs (broad-leafed weeds) and twigs off the trees." The deer and antelope will also forage for bark and acorns.

Walking through the large pastures of the Broken Arrow Ranch late in the afternoon, perfumes of cedar and oak trees permeate the air. Perrin Wells, general manager of the Broken Arrow Ranch and a specialist on herbs and plants, explains that the "aromas of leafy plants in dry areas tend to be a little stronger" and have a direct effect on the venison. "We've noticed that when a deer eats a lot of leaves from the juniper tree, it has more of that taste." Several local freshwater springs also release an array of earthy scents.

"As a result, the meat has a more complex flavor than an animal living on a pasture of just one type of grass," Hughes states.

When the evening comes, cooling the air and wrapping the ranch in shadow, deer approach the gardens surrounding Hughes's house for moonlight grazing. Hughes's smooth voice settles out the window into the evening breeze as he tells the legend behind the ranch's name.

"The legend of Broken Arrow recalls an ancient ritual of respect between two Native Americans," Hughes narrates. "Upon meeting, an arrow was broken in half to represent the truth, peace, and friendship that was to forever dwell between them," Hughes sits back on the porch and breathes in the brisk air. An apt adage, befitting the ranch where people and animals have come to dwell together in peace and prosperity, as tradition would have it.

"Serve it roasted, braised, or with a sauce."

JEAN-LOUIS PALLADIN

MUSHROOMS

Wild, wild mushrooms

Among the soft clouds of billowing mist that blanket the mountains between Oregon and Washington, wild mushrooms grow as fast as the rain falls. Tiny parasols of velvety brown and white sprout year round against a mural of forests, snow-capped mountains, and waterfalls. Venturing into this beauty, hundreds of people hope to find and savor one of the luxurious mushrooms—the elusive chanterelle, perhaps, or the woodsy morel.

Charles Novy is one of those people, though his quest has gone several steps further. Nearly twenty years ago in Vancouver, Washington, he established the company Fresh and Wild. Since then, he has provided restaurants across America with a selection of the best and wildest wild mushrooms in North America.

Born in Ohio, Novy pulled his first mushroom, a candy cap, in a neighbor's front yard when he was just twelve years old. "It was a very easy one to identify, and I had seen it in a book," Novy confesses now, nearly a half-century later. He asked his mother to cook it and, to his surprise, she did. "It was terrific." Novy laughs, still astonished, and adds that he doesn't know who was braver, he or his mother, to actually eat the specimen. From there, Novy began to develop his knowledge of the mushroom. It wasn't until he entered his forties, however, that Novy, a research chemist, would begin to devote his professional life to toadstools and truffles.

When Novy first moved to Oregon, he enjoyed hiking and backpacking in the spring. "I found all these fresh morels growing everywhere," he remembers as if just returning from his first jaunt into the mountains. "So I started picking them and called a chef in Pennsylvania to see if I could sell them." The chef advised Novy to sell his mushrooms only to the best restaurants if he wanted to be fairly compensated. The chef warned, however, that it was unlikely that Novy could make a living from doing so. Intent on having his passion succeed as a business, Novy went ahead and launched his company. He has since become a leading expert on delectable saprophytes.

And he features many: cepes, hedgehogs, morels, black trumpets, yellowfoot, lobster, chicken of the woods, matsutake, and black-and-white chanterelles. Novy sends a staff of foragers to collect the best varieties on the continent—from the Pacific mountains down to the coast, and from Canada to northern California.

Patty Weihl, who works for Fresh and Wild, outlines the spectrum of delectable little sprouts. In the summer and fall, the Pacific Northwest chanterelle, prized for its "cheerful golden color," has a flavor reminiscent of apricot and pumpkin. In the winter, the black trumpet is popular for its "fragrant and fruity" taste.

Frequently, mushrooms share two, if not more, different names. The cepe mushroom, for example, is also known as the porcini, "little pig" in Italian, for its plump meat and smoky aroma. Names are also evocative of the toadstools' shape or texture. The chicken of the woods is termed for its flavor and consistency which resembles chicken breast, while the maple cap, found under pine and oak trees, offers a sweet maple bouquet that is enhanced when dried.

Novy makes it clear that "to go up and down all day long, and walk those hills until you eventually find some wonderful mushrooms," patience is not of paramount importance but, rather, a strong set of legs.

Novy describes one of his favorite mushrooms, the matsutake, which requires both physical stamina and patience to locate. Also known as the pine mushroom, it is a white growth bearing a spicy aroma and a cinnamon flavor. Highly valued, the quest for the mushroom has become epic.

"People would hunt the matsutake at night with miners' lights strapped around the head," Novy tells. After harvesting them, these people then covered up the overturned ground so that the next person passing by wouldn't see the white mushroom coming through. Even today, harvesters place little patches on the spots where the mushroom has been plucked, draw maps of the area, and sell the information for a profit. It has even been rumored that people carry guns while harvesting the plant, prepared to use deadly force if necessary to obtain the little pod.

"It's just a legend," stresses Novy who adds, on a more serious note, that carrying a gun in the woods is actually wise considering the bears, cougars, and mountain lions that inhabit the region. Sold anywhere from $10 to $100 per pound, the price matsutake commands reflects its overwhelming demand.

While mushrooms have different tastes and textures, they all deserve to be carefully cooked. Novy learned this important lesson the hard way while living in New Jersey years ago. "I had picked, from the base of oak trees, honey mushrooms in a cluster. The cluster was so big that I had to take all my food out of the refrigerator just to fit it in." That night, Novy cooked the honey mushroom over smoked trout, "very lightly broiled." By midnight, he awoke terribly ill and eventually passed out. Upon recovering, "I wondered if I had eaten a dangerous one, so I got out all my mushroom books and started reading about the symptoms. Since it affected me so quickly, I concluded that it was not a serious matter, because mushroom poisoning takes much longer after ingestion."

Still, Novy knows that he should have cooked his mushroom longer. After all, mushrooms are the roses of fungi, and their beauty can carry a prick if not handled carefully like the flowers they often appear to be.

"Shave raw mushrooms with a mandoline and make a salad of mushrooms, celery, and good old parmesan. Serve with bread and olive oil, what else could you ask for?"

ALESSANDRO STRATTA

OLIVE OIL

A woman and a dream

The sun still has two hours before it sets over Napa Valley, California. Peggy O'Kelly, founder of the St. Helena Olive Oil Company, and her friend and colleague, Kelly McElearney, decide to have a look at the olives nearly ready for harvest. Ripe and firm, the olives will be used for the latest addition to her line of products—olive oil from Napa Valley.

The olive trees rest on top of a hill located between St. Helena and Pope Valley. Growing on the edges of numerous vineyards, the graceful trees frame a spectacular landscape. O'Kelly walks on the property, plucks a plump specimen from a tree, and inspects the fruit. Its brown exterior and white, purple-veined interior satisfy her. "We will harvest these trees in two weeks," she says, adding that the olives will be handpicked to avoid bruising.

Napa Valley olive trees are more than one hundred and fifty years old. As McElearney explains, Franciscan priests first brought the seeds to California from Mexico and planted them in the late 1700s. The Spaniards quickly learned that the soil and climate provided optimal conditions for growing olive trees and pressed the oil for their own consumption in the early 1800s. "By 1885, olive growers in California were making oils that could compete with the imported ones."

Over the course of the nineteenth century, olive production boomed in Modesto and the Central Valley, while in Napa Valley, most of the trees remained simply for their aesthetic appeal. Over time, however, the demand for olive oil declined in light of the high cost of production. Not until the 1960s and 70s, when the "gourmandizing" of olive oil began, did America rediscover its treasure. Then, O'Kelly claims, Napa Valley landowners cut back their fruit orchards to accommodate the scattered olive trees, pruned them, and started collecting olive oil.

The inaugural bottles from her first harvest stand proudly on a table in her local warehouse on the outskirts of St. Helena. Made from a blend of different types of olives -- Leccino, Sevillano, Frantoio, Pendolino, Coratina, and Manzanillo -- the olives were picked from the Pedegral Vineyards Estate and cold-pressed that same day. While the names reflect southern Europe, the oils are, unquestionably, products of Napa Valley sun.

"No one, but Kelly and I, have tasted it yet," O'Kelly says pointing to the octagonal bottle containing the pale amber liquid. A sample of the oil brings a surprisingly robust green apple flavor to the mouth for the first few seconds, then resonates in a uniquely pungent, somewhat bittersweet taste.

CRANBERRY

BERRY
BALSAMIC

*Fresh native tart
cranberries & vanilla were
combined with
Balsamic Vinegar
of Modena*

ST. HELENA
OLIVE OIL CO.

"This is gold to us," O'Kelly says, although she won't be able to produce more than 30 gallons a year for the first few years. Mass production of the oil is implausible in light of the economic and proprietary dominance of the Napa Valley vineyards. According to St. Helena Olive Oil Company, while one ton of grapes yields about 180 gallons of wine, the same amount of olives will yield only about 27 gallons of oil. And while the price of the land in Napa Valley is high -- ranging from $75,000 to $200,000 per acre -- it can cost $40 per gallon to produce an extra virgin olive oil, McElearney explains. Still, because of the oil's very specific qualities, O'Kelly hopes to compete at the highest international level.

"Another great thing is that the olives are crushed and cold-pressed no more than an hour and a-half after they have been picked. You do everything you can to get the olives into the bin without bruising them and get them to the crusher as soon as possible," she says.

O'Kelly is enamored with her trade. A single mother of two, she had tired of her daily commute to San Francisco as a business woman. With the help of her brother, chef Jeffrey Jake, she launched the St. Helena Olive Oil Company. O'Kelly attended lectures by experts from Italy, Spain, and France, who provided her with the necessary European know-how, "I learned how to taste olive oil, how to pick olives, and how to crush them."

In addition to the Napa Valley Olive Oil, O'Kelly produces a series of three different olive oils for a total production of 2,400 cases per year. She also makes a variety of vinegars, including a unique champagne vinegar made from champagne that still sparkles (most champagne vinegars are made with champagne that has lost its effervescence).

"We do everything in house, and we don't want anybody else in the process," O'Kelly expresses, adding that while she will never become a huge producer, she will be pleased just to create high-quality products.

She brings forward a bottle of 100 percent extra virgin oil made of Sevillano olives. "The later you harvest the olives, the softer the flavor of the fruits," she says. The Sevillano olive oil releases a certain rich subtlety, quite distinct from the Napa Valley oil. As it rests on the tongue, a full, yet mild, tangy flavor lingers on. A Tuscan touch to a very Californian product.

"I love olive oil on a toasted slice of bread with fleur de sel."

JEAN-LOUIS PALLADIN

POULTRY

Musical squab

Music envelopes Manuel Thomas's squab farm in Turlock, California, south of Modesto. Broadcasted from white speakers planted throughout the estate, songs play from every angle into the rows of wide birdcages. A visitor, having been informed that this is one of the busiest squab farms in the country, may suppose that the purpose of the music is to maintain a certain working rigor. Not exactly, of the people that is.

Thomas, who has farmed here since 1972, explains that the music soothes the pigeons, whose offspring are the young nestling birds known as squab, and creates a buffer from disturbing sounds. Joanne Bettencourt, who works with Thomas, approves of the modern serenade. "I know a farmer who broadcasts tunes from the 1940s. I told him that I could hear his birds snoring," she laughs. Working assiduously, Thomas foregoes his own calm in order to ensure a stress-free environment for the pigeons breeding his squab.

"The veal of poultry," as squab is called by Bob Shipley, head of the cooperative Squab Producers of California, the small birds have been enjoyed as a culinary delight for centuries and are popular in Asia, the Middle East, and Europe. Despite its delicate texture and flavor, Shipley estimates that 85 percent of all Americans do not really know what squab is. Even those who do, rarely prepare it at home.

Yet, squab has found success in California. The squab farming community near Modesto is comprised of more than 70 small farms which share an 11,000-square-foot, state-of-the-art processing facility. Built in 1983, and completely remodeled since, the plant itself tells the story of squab farmers who fought doggedly to keep the bird a viable market product.

In the late 1930s, farmers raised squab primarily for the Chinese community in the San Francisco Bay area. The market was limited, however. "In those days the markets were live markets," explains Shipley. "Buyers owned booths in the marketplace and collaborated to force the squab price down to a low level." By the summer of 1934, "squab was flooding the market at 35 cents per pound," wrote John Smith, one of the founders of the squab cooperative.

In response to the squab market crash, farmers joined together to organize the cooperative. As the initial step, farmers brought the birds to the market in one truck instead of several separate ones. "They announced, 'take it or leave it, this is our price,'" Shipley says, telling the story. The organization survived and, today, 700,000 to 800,000 birds are processed every year and sent nationwide.

Thomas is one of the successful members of the cooperative. Carrying several different breeds of pigeons, he nurtures approximately 2,200 pairs and their progeny. Walking through the numerous corridors of his farm, the sixty-five-year-old farmer highlights the methods he employs in creating the ideal conditions for breeding premium squab. In addition to the music, during the winter months he simulates a fourteen-hour period of daylight. "The pigeons make love during the day," Thomas explains with a warm smile. And fourteen hours is ample time to promote the necessary cooing and cuddling.

Indeed, "amour" is at the core of squab farming. Pigeons are monogamous creatures and at age five to six months will find a mate with which they pair for life. Shipley calls these mature birds "mum" and "dad." Their purpose is, quite naturally, to mate and reproduce as often as possible. The farmer's purpose, therefore, is to provide the birds with the consummate environment in which to do just that. "If the birds are not happy," Shipley says, "they are not doing their jobs." Plainly put, mood is everything.

Thomas steps to the side of a pen and stands over a nest which is virtually clogged with the birds' manure. As in the wild, the birds pack their nests with their own manure to warm the interior and provide a protective barrier. Nests are cleaned only when the manure blocks its entrance, typically once a year.

He reaches in and grasps a young Red Carneau, a crossbreed descended from French and Swiss pigeons and the American White King pigeon. He wets his thumb and gently runs it up against the squab's breast, ruffling the plume. A feather comes loose and he examines small droplets of blood resting on its point. From the prick of blood, Thomas can tell the exact age of the bird.

"This one is thirty-one days old," he says matter-of-factly and delicately returns the bird to its pen. Since young squab are selected within twenty-six to thirty-two days of hatching, Thomas has to quickly decide whether the bird will be sent to the processing plant or remain to be matched with another bird as a mum or dad. About 25 percent of the birds are kept for breeding purposes. The oldest birds, which, after five years of mating are no longer as productive as they once were, are replaced each year.

Once paired, the couples are placed into a pen containing two boxes of six bi-leveled nests, or lodges. "They are very territorial," says Shipley, amused at the unexpected character trait that requires separating the nests. After having settled in their dens, the birds are fed, according to Thomas, "the best corn in the country." Thomas and other farmers belonging to the local cooperative feed the pigeons with corn grown in the San Joaquin Delta located on the fringe of San Francisco Bay. "Pigeons are very selective with what they eat, so we provide them with cafeteria-style meals of the best grain, and they just eat what they like."

A carefully calculated diet and natural environment are only some of the factors that make the California squab so succulent. The Central Valley weather, a warm summer followed by a cool but calm winter, allows the farmers to raise the birds outdoors and without artificial heat. "As control, we just put plastic around the cages in the winter to protect against sporadic frost or morning fog," Shipley points out.

Other key qualities of the California squab are its excellent genetic lines. Squab Producers of California have crossbred a variety of unusual pigeons. For example, the Hubble pigeon, a mix of the Mondaine and

White King pigeons, is neither large nor active. "So it has been crossed with broad-breasted, more active birds in order to increase its vitality," Thomas explains. He can recognize the individual breed by the size of the bird's beak and the plumage, which ranges in color from purple to white.

Once warm and well-fed, mum lays two eggs about eight to ten times a year. She and dad incubate the eggs for about three weeks until they hatch. The feeding process is also shared between the parent pigeons. "The first several days, they regurgitate a pigeon milk, or crop milk—an enzymatic blend of the bird's saliva and feed," says Thomas.

After being exclusively fed by mum and dad for several days, the squab then receive a mash of whole grain corn, wheat, and milo. "We also feed them pellets, a special high protein blend of natural grains such as soy and alfalfa."

When twenty-six days old, the chicks are nudged out of the nests and into the world by the parent birds. "At that point, when they are out of the nest and just about to fly, squabs are harvested for the market," says Shipley, who refuses to say he kills the birds. Since the birds have never flown, the muscles are tender, full, and still quite young.

"Hopefully mum has already laid two more eggs, and the cycle has started over again," Thomas concludes earnestly. By then, he'll have new music playing down the halls in stereo.

"Boil a flavored stock according to tastes, immerse the squabs, and lower the fire. Cover the casserole and let the bird cook for twenty minutes."

SYLVAIN PORTAY

Milk-fed poulardes

As farmers, Sylvia and Stephen Pryzant continuously challenge themselves to raise animals in the most effective, albeit often unusual, manner. Today, on their farm in Honesdale, Pennsylvania, the couple fosters a particular fascination with milk-fed *poulardes* or young female chickens.

Following the farming methods of the Bresse region of France, the Pryzants began to milk-feed their clutch of *poulardes* in 1997. A rare practice since, according to Sylvia, "it is very hard to raise poultry on milk as it is by nature lactose intolerant." Yet, the Pryzants have managed to complete the task by employing a simple trade secret. They mix the milk with mashed corn.

In the barn, the young chicks run to the feed troughs and eagerly swallow the white creamy meal. In so doing, the animals not only benefit from the milk, but from the qualities of the natural grain. The effect is readily visible in the birds' appearance. Their faces assume a pale pink flush while their plumage, in telling display, takes on a golden, cornsilk color.

"I am a strong believer that what you put in the animal, you will get out of the product," Sylvia says.

Fed with milk, the *poularde* develops a lighter, moister meat and bears a delicate flavor, finer than that of regular chicken. The poularde is generally recognizable for its lack of a comb and wattle dangling from its chin (the telltale signs of chicken masculinity). Not yet sexually mature, the birds remain too young to lay eggs.

The animals arrive at the farm soon after hatching, where they will remain feeding on milk for approximately nine weeks. In that time, they develop a full breast and robust thighs. The Pryzants chose to raise the Cornish *poularde*, a white-feathered variety, specifically because it has been "bred to be plumper and meatier than a regular chicken," chats Sylvia while wandering through the farm with her husband. As she picks up some manure from the ground to inspect, Stephen feigns an offended expression. Before he can say a word, however, she interjects, "Come on! It's nature." After playful banter, Stephen explains that the manure, "is actually a guideline that tells you how the birds are converting their food into body weight and whether they're healthy."

Somewhat delicate creatures, the birds often respond negatively to varying weather patterns. "They can be stressed out because some days will be nice and others cold," Sylvia says. Such temperature swings

The best known of all poultry is undoubtedly the chicken, specifically, the young, not yet sexually mature rooster or hen. A castrated rooster, known as a capon, will get fatter than other mature roosters. Raised free-range or fed inside a barn, the tastes and textures of chicken vary. At the Four Story Hill Farm in Honesdale, Pennsylvania, the Pryzants have patiently learned how to raise female chickens, poulardes, by feeding them a milk-based preparation.

have a direct impact on the birds' appetite and weight. The animals will suddenly stop eating, then, in equally abrupt fashion, resume feeding.

Living in closed quarters helps to protect the poulardes from the extreme outdoor temperatures, therefore making it easier for the birds to maintain their weight.

Enjoying the success of their poulardes, the couple is now boldly considering raising chickens on pasture grass, a completely different product with a completely different taste. To do so, however, the Pryzants would need to stop milk-feeding the poulardes—a craft, having been perfected, they are unlikely to forsake.

"Poularde: Roast it with ventreche (lard), garlic, sarriette (savory), and roasted potatoes."

JEAN-LOUIS PALLADIN

Seasons of the pheasant

Mud and wet snow cover the ground of the large open pen. Inside, nearly wild male pheasants move about in agitated, if not aggressive, manner. It is late winter, the most difficult, yet highly critical, season for raising pheasants. In another nearby open pen, hen-pheasants await their male counterparts for battle. Breeding, that is.

Large and wild, pheasants do not lead serene lives. Raised outside, the birds are violent animals, often cannibalistic, and some of the hardest fowl to raise. A task that George Rude, President of Criggstown Farm in New Jersey, has assumed since 1975.

"I hunt a lot," Rude says simply, justifying his passion for pheasants and quail, his other farm-raised product. Since the commercial sale of hunted fowl is illegal, Rude launched a farm on his 80-acre estate near Princeton to professionalize his hobby. Today, he produces a bird bearing rich, gamy, and intensely flavored meat. Regal in appearance, with a white, narrow ring encircling the neck and brilliantly colored plumage, the pheasant, once served as the culinary centerpiece in Medieval royal dining halls, has long been enjoyed as one of the most luxurious birds.

To raise his pheasants, Rude has devised a calendar in which the seasons start slightly earlier than those of the regular year. Spring, according to Rude, begins in early March and marks the onset of the breeding season. He has re-created a natural environment inside the outdoor pens where pheasants reproduce with a male to female ratio of 1 to 12. Although July is considered the last breeding month, Rude calls the party off as early as June. "By then, we will have all the birds we need," he says. Moreover, since the males are aggressive in their mating habits, by the end of spring, "the hens are real beat up."

Throughout the course of the mating season, the hens lay approximately one egg every thirty hours. As such, "a hen will give birth to an average of 27 chicks from start to finish," Rude estimates.

After hatching, the young pheasants are raised indoors for the first six days. During this early period, Rude monitors the feather growth and size of the chicks to determine when they have matured enough to be transferred outside. Once ready for the switch, the still-juvenile birds are placed into the open-aired pens. Within six weeks time, however, protective plastic guards called peepers are then attached to the young birds' beaks in order to prevent wounding from the inevitable fighting with other pheasants. In summer, which extends from June to August, more than 2,000 pheasants fly about within the large pens which are covered broadly with loose arching nets.

Thinly separated from the nearby fields, corn stalks and sorghum -- a variety of Old World grass that produces a seed commonly used in stock feed -- grow inside the pens in close imitation of a natural environment. Rude is quick to qualify, however, "I am a poultry raiser," and adds, "we don't harvest that corn." The vegetation in the pens also has concealing purposes. Many pheasants seek cover and protection under the broad-leafed plants from the more aggressive birds. "They also need that cover for the rain and the hot elements . . . just as if they were in the wild," Rude adds. On bare, exposed land, the animal would not likely survive.

The corn, although sometimes protective, does not always allow Rude to keep an eye on his birds. Predators find their way in through certain breaks in the netting. One night, Rude recalls, a raccoon mother snuck her four cubs into the pen for the sole apparent reason of teaching them how to hunt. While 400 pheasants were killed, none were taken for food.

Rude's attempt to replicate the open air by using high nets allows the birds to exercise freely and vigorously as though living in its unconstrained habitat. As a result, the animals' red meat maintains the same wild qualities found in completely feral specimens. The high-protein diet pheasants require maintains their considerable bulk and makes them one of the heaviest of all game birds, explains Rude, who also sells his product for hunting purposes.

Harvesting signals the beginning of the autumn season, usually starting with the month of September. At eighteen weeks, the pheasants are brought into a long alley and captured with a net. Throughout the course of the fall, a total of 35,000 pheasants are harvested. The first hatch of pheasants, born in early spring, are singled out and kept for breeding into the next mating season. They await winter in the pen.

These pheasants are oblivious to the snow and cold. But when January and February approach, shortening the days and turning the soil winter-gray, the restless birds sense the breeding season just a month away. And, then, only night and darkness keep them calm and quiet.

"Roast the pheasant in the oven, very simply, in a smelting casserole. At the end, add vegetables and fruits in season."

ALAIN DUCASSE

Muscovy duck

Of the three domestic ducks raised in the United States -- the Pekin, the Muscovy, and the Moulard -- the Muscovy duck is uncontested for yielding the most succulent meat. With smooth, delicate, and lean breasts and thighs and velvety foie gras, the Muscovy, also known as the *Canard de Barbarie*, has found its place in the American palate.

A bird of Argentinian origin, the Muscovy is a relatively recent introduction to the United States, available only since the 1980s. Much of its popularity is due, in large part, to the efforts of Claude Bigo, a Frenchman who distributed duck throughout France in 1985, before coming to work at Grimaud Farms in Stockton, California, in 1985. Over the past fifteen years, he has persevered in successfully raising what was at first considered an uncommon variety of duck. Today he markets entire hens, or *canette*, either uncooked or baked according to southwestern French tradition. One such preparation is the *confit de canard*—duck's thigh which has been cooked slowly in its own fat. An absolute delicacy, the tender meat simply melts off the bone.

While savoring duck meat is effortless, raising the animal is not. "Because this duck has less fat, it is more difficult to raise," Bigo explains. "It needs warmer temperatures than other ducks." The warm summerlike temperatures of Stockton provide the ideal environment for Bigo to house the hundreds of birds in Louisiana-style barns—open structures with wide-paneled windows and shutters. "We can play with the shutters, thus creating an impression of daylight and exterior," explains Olivier Rochard, another Frenchman who joined Grimaud Farms in order to supervise production. The temperate, airy and natural environment of the barns improves the overall quality of the birds' health and, ultimately, their meat. Standing in one of the seven Grimaud barns, Rochard inspects a few of the 3,000 seven-day-old yellow ducklings. "We try to maintain a 78° temperature," he explains while carefully observing the young chicks eating cereals and soy, and drinking water. Hens (females), and drakes (males), are kept together and reproduce naturally. Treated with neither antibiotics nor hormones, the birds take longer to reach maturity and produce a sweeter, higher-quality meat.

The requests for Muscovy have reached the point that Bigo can no longer satisfy all orders. To accommodate the increased market, another Grimaud Farm has been planned in Pennsylvania where he intends to also raise Moulard ducks, a cross between the Pekin and Muscovy. While Bigo controls his California duck farm, his responsibilities at the new location will be delegated to Pennsylvania farmers. This suits Bigo just fine. Since the Muscovy has indeed become an American specialty, it rests well in the hands of American farmers.

Before roasting the duck, I marinate it with balsamic vinegar, olive oil, and ground black pepper. This will caramelize and flavor the duck during the roasting process

RENÉ BAJEUX

156

Yet, his enterprise had to be started from scratch. He and his new partner launched a company called Commonwealth, where they controlled the entire process from breeding to slaughter.

Yanay favored the Moulard duck over geese because of the fine quality foie gras it produces as well as the breed's innate resistance to disease. Although he succeeded in raising the ducks almost immediately, Yanay says that his partner found it nearly impossible to sell a product that many chefs were not accustomed to preparing. Almost as soon as they started, the two men lost 5,000 livers.

"So I tried to sell the livers myself," says Yanay. Wearing his work clothes and carrying samples of his cream-colored foie gras, he drove to New York and stopped at every upscale restaurant. "But without success," Yanay recalls. "Nobody wanted to even look at it."

Then, as fate would have it, he met a young Frenchwoman who inquired where he had found his foie gras. "I was very surprised that she could even pronounce the word properly," chuckles Yanay. Upon chatting with her, he discovered that the woman, Ariane Daguin, was the daughter of the well-known French chef André Daguin. With a shared expertise, they struck up an alliance—he would provide the foie gras, and she would sell it.

Soon after their meeting, Daguin opened D'Artagnan, a company specializing in the distribution of foie gras and other poultry delicacies. Daguin began to visit restaurants and explain to chefs the proper handling of foie gras, which was still relatively unknown in the United States. "When the chefs saw the white foie gras, they thought it was cooked," Yanay says, amused. Slowly, however, sales were made and business began to move forward.

Real success for Yanay, however, commenced when he left Commonwealth and, in 1992, joined Ginor, an American who had completed his military service in Israel, in creating Hudson Valley Foie Gras in Upstate New York's Sullivan County. Ginor's passion, it could be said, matches that of his partner.

"I have spent the last ten years consumed by this venture, spreading the 'foie gras gospel,' to anybody who will listen," wrote Ginor in the introduction of his book, *Foie Gras, A Passion*. Yet the book, published in 1999, stirred a controversy in New York when the Smithsonian Institution organized a special event at which Ginor was scheduled to speak. Animal advocates made public complaints and the lecture was canceled.

While protest to gavage exists, the counterargument stands that since the birds are waterfowl -- long distance travelers -- they are accustomed to heavy consumption. Duck and geese often eat more food than necessary and store large amounts of fat to sustain themselves during their long migrations. Yanay contends that through gavage, people have simply emphasized this natural, biological aspect of the animal.

Pursuant to studies conducted in France, Yanay says, while ducks produce corticosterone, a substance often related to stress, during the first two days of hand-feeding, the corticosterone disappears as the birds adjust to the gavage. He adds, "actually some ducks want to have a little more food right after they are fed."

On Yanay's farm, ducks roam outside and flap about in the cold winter weather. "You acclimate the ducks to the cold because they will eat more and grow better," Yanay points out. At the age of 13 weeks of life, gavage starts as ducks are hand-fed a corn mixture three times a day. A woman, carrying a feeder, moves from cage to cage and handles each bird individually. Gavage continues for approximately thirty days, or until the duck weighs about 16 to 17 pounds. Once killed and bled, the animal is cooled for sixteen hours before the liver is removed. At that point, the liver is firm, smooth and clean of blood.

Prepared as a *terrine* or sauteed, foie gras has become a favorite choice in American restaurants. Still, Yanay is frustrated that duck meat, itself, remains unknown by the American public. *Confit de Moulard,* duck thighs that have been slowly cooked in their own fat, and the *Magret de Canard,* duck breast often confused with beef due to its red meat, are some of France's most popular dishes. Duck fat is also used to cook succulent potatoes, as well as the birds' gizzards and neck. Yet, for now, Yanay is pleased to finally see an American passion for a product that has been enjoyed by European countries for centuries. Appreciation for the rest of the duck will surely likewise follow.

"Either prepare the foie gras as a terrine, with salt and pepper, or wholly roasted and served on toasted country bread. Serve it lightly peppered, with fresh grapes.

LAURENT MANRIQUE

SHELLFISH

A day off the coast of Maine

The road from Portland to Spruce Head Island, Maine, has plenty of surprises in store for those who have never visited northern New England. At times, a calm sea can emerge from the cresting hills with endless peacefulness. Yet, winter storms often pound the shore and, as testament to the sea's frequent fury, the oldest houses are crowned with widow's walks from which women, years ago, would watch for their husbands' return from sea. On their small fishing boat, Richard Lowell, Merton Sawyer, and Doug Pennington joke about this foreboding architectural feature while trying to fix a sudden breakdown of the outboard engine.

Eventually, the engine turns and the men leave Spruce Head's small bay for a day of fishing—as they do every day, weather permitting. The boat is probably the smallest of the armada leaving the docks, but the mens' diving equipment boasts sizable ambition: to handpick, in frigid waters, the best shellfish available that Rod Mitchell at Browne Trading Company has asked them to harvest.

The men met early that morning. After working together for several years, they operate like a perfectly synchronized machine and load the boat with wet suits and tanks in a matter of minutes. Now underway, Lowell, the captain, sails straight to his favorite urchin spots as the other men dress in thick gear.

"I know where to find urchins because of my experience," Lowell, who has been a fisherman for more than thirty years, says over the loud drone of the engine. Assisted by a computer installed in the boat's cabin, he has been able to trace the urchin hot spots. The computer also helps him to navigate the ocean floor and locate large clusters of kelp, the urchins' main food source, where, as Lowell puts it, "they like to hang out."

Standing in 22° wind, the men plunge their gloves into boiling water to warm them up before diving into the 28° water. Bundled in vulcanized rubber suits, they slip into the icy embrace of the sea where they will stay underwater for at least ten minutes before surfacing with bags full of urchins. In the winter, the water actually gets warmer the further they dive, reaching 32° at its deepest point.

In the past, collecting urchins required just a simple swim across the ocean bottom as thousands of the spiky animals scattered the North Atlantic floor. Lowell remembers the time when a solitary diver would harvest 2,000 pounds of urchins in one day. Due to considerable fishing, however, the population has decreased to the point that a catch of 400 to 500 pounds a day is a success.

"What makes a good urchin is its yellow color and the amount of roe," explains Richard Lowell, the captain of a small vessel in the North Atlantic. Accompanying him on the boat are scuba divers Doug Pennington and Merton Sawyer (top left), who remember a scary day diving. Upon discovering a dense collection of urchins, one of the divers got carried away and failed to keep track of the time. When he finally came to the surface, the boat was steaming away, leaving him behind. He floated for hours. By the time the boat returned to retrieve him, he was nearly unconscious. Despite the dangers, both men love diving and seem impatient to get back into the water for the hunt.

Sawyer resurfaces first. He hands Lowell his bag and disappears again beneath the glassy water as smoothly as a seal. Lowell takes an urchin out of the bag and, very delicately, turns it in his gloved hand. The only way to determine the quality of the catch is to sample a few.

"What makes a good urchin is the yellow color and the amount of the roe," Lowell explains while cutting one in half. He looks down at the split creature, a slight whistle parting his mouth. While the animal has the desirable yellow color, the roe is sparse. He throws it aside. After discarding an undersized urchin, he breaks open a third and turns his face down critically, "that's a real bad color, reddish, that's real bad." Judging this stock to be low quality, he throws the remaining contents of the bag overboard.

"Good urchins depend on the time of the year and the amount of kelp they have been eating," Lowell says, noting that cold waters induce the urchin to spawn.

Looking out over the sea, he waits for the divers to produce another bag for inspection. In order to preserve the animal's reproductive cycle, harvesting is permitted only between the months of October and February. Laughingly, Lowell admits that he doesn't even really like to eat urchin, "it's too sweet for me."

Pennington and Sawyer eventually climb aboard with urchins good enough to take to Mitchell. They eagerly talk about the diving conditions, like young men returning from a sporting event which they had won.

"Tide is coming in, the current was pretty strong on this exposed ledge," remarks Sawyer, wiping his face through a wide smile.

"Tide was pretty good for me," echoes Pennington. "It was like swimming in a river, swimming *upstream* in a river I should say."

Their tanks allow them to stay forty-five minutes to an hour underwater and they regularly go through four tanks per day. Only strong winds that cloud the ocean prevent them from completing their dives. Otherwise, through rain or snow, they go out and under.

While diving remains a very dangerous job, it is "exciting" and "adventurous," assert both Pennington and Sawyer. One of the difficulties of diving in cold, deep waters is the ability to remain steady against the powerful currents of the ocean bottom in order to collect the urchins one by one and place them in the bags.

When enough urchins are gathered, Lowell navigates to a position further out where scallops can be found in waters 60 to 70 feet deep. Scallops generally live anywhere from ten to 300 feet, but divers do not usually swim below 100 feet due to decompression problems. It's early December, the beginning of the scallop season, which runs through April, and the shellfish are at their best in the cold waters. During the summer months, when the water warms and scallops begin to spawn, the meat tends to be tougher and not as flavorful.

There are two ways to harvest scallops. The most common method is "dragging" where a large net is pulled along the ocean floor. But Mitchell, who distributes the scallops, does not approve of this method. "This type of scallop, caught with the net, lives deeper in a muddy bottom where there are fewer rocks," Mitchell notes. He explains further that when they are brought up, the shells often break, the animal is stressed, and it dies before even reaching the deck. As a result, the shellfish will not be fresh once served on a plate.

Oysters, from coast to coast

Almost all categories of foods come in a melee of varieties, bearing the unique flavors, textures, and scents of the regions from which they originate. The oyster, with its many diverse lines, is one of the animals most sensitive to environment. Therefore, America, with its expansive bodies of water, varying temperatures and fertile climates, yields a dizzying array of oysters with distinctively bold and luxuriant flavors.

Despite their complexity, the secret to cultivating prime oysters is mystifyingly simple, claims Michael Watchorn, an oyster farmer in Marshall, California. "All it takes, is to make the oyster happy," he says. "We give them as much room as possible. In desperate times, we talk to them," he jests. "They'd think we're crazy."

Off the shores of Marshall, large floating bags are visible where the shellfish grow in protected fashion. At low tide, the sacs slowly rise to the surface, exposing the oysters to the sun and fresh California air. When the tide is high, the bags sink down again about six feet below the surface. Throughout the ebb and flow, the shellfish continuously open and close their shells to exercise and rinse away debris.

Watchorn pulls out some specimens, "these are very nice, and the shells are deep cupped," he explains. "The rich colors -- purple, green, and black -- mean they're healthy. Otherwise they'd be real bleached out."

The most difficult task in eating oysters is selecting which one: the Pacific oyster, the Atlantic oyster, the Japanese Kumamoto, the European Belon, or one of the several other varieties. Watchorn opens a Japanese Kumamoto, a small, tender oyster. A breed originating in Japanese waters, the shellfish has a buttery, sweet, even fruity taste, not as salty as most Atlantic oysters. Watchorn recommends the Kumamoto for oyster novices, "it's a real forgiving oyster for first-time oyster eaters—those who don't like the texture of it." He walks over to a deck and looks over the bay.

"There are two essential elements in farming oysters," Watchorn softly contemplates under the unexpected winter sun, "purity of the water and proximity to a market."

Back in the early 1980s, Watchorn and his partners established a small oyster farm, Hog Island Oyster Company, deep in Marshall's wilderness. A marine sanctuary, Marshall has no industrial development to contaminate the bay. Only the tumultuous weather's frequent waves, which prevent the free-swimming larvae from settling and developing their shells, pose a concern. Nonetheless, Watchorn's choice in area proved a smart one—soon after he settled, oyster bars became the craze in nearby San Francisco.

Crawfish, the Cajun star

In 1952, Pat Huval bought a hamburger stand and an adjoining dance hall in the tiny, unknown town of Henderson, Louisiana. Featuring Cajun crawfish and hamburgers, the small stand grew as quickly as the booming town around it. By the early 1970s, Henderson was on the American map, and Huval had become its mayor. Step-by-step, Huval, who remained mayor for nearly twenty years, expanded his restaurant enterprise into a small faux-village known as The Fisherman's Wharf. Proudly Cajun, Huval continues to serve, as his specialty, Louisiana's richest culinary treasure: crawfish.

"Back in the late 1940s, crawfish wasn't popular," explains Huval speaking in a mixed tongue of French, Cajun, and English. "Catfish was my best-seller until crawfish became popular in the late 1950s. Since then, we've grown together," he laughs.

Huval cooks the crawfish in numerous ways: boiled, fried, à l'étouffée (simmered in a Cajun stew and served over rice), as a bisque, as a gumbo, or stuffed with bell pepper. Each time, he cooks it his own way with secret know-how, "a little bit of this, a little bit of that, I taste it and when I say 'Mummm,' I know it's good. That's Cajun cooking." The big man grins from ear to ear.

Although Huval harvests wild crawfish from the nearby Amy River, he also buys the shellfish from his longtime friend, another proud Cajun, Roy Robin. The two men first met when Huval was selling gumbo from his restaurant-dance hall. They bonded over the southern specialty, which both appreciated as a legendary cure for hangovers. Huval hums its virtues as though singing an old refrain.

When it's cold, you eat gumbo,
get the gogo (woman),
and get to dodo (bed)

As Huval developed his restaurant, Robin specialized in harvesting crawfish and launched his own business, Bayou Land Seafood.

Swimming in the multitude of Louisiana bayous, crawfish can be caught in the wild or farmed in natural ponds. With a distinctive taste, slightly stronger than lobster, the shellfish has a devoted following of people willing to go through the pains of peeling the tiny animal for just a small mouthful of meat. While 100 pounds of shrimp will produce 60 pounds of meat, the same amount of crawfish will produce only 16 pounds. On average, Robin harvests approximately 3.5 million pounds of crawfish each year.

Raising the tastiest crawfish requires large expanses of land, high-quality water, and concentrated work. "It's a tough job," Robin admits. "A short day is twelve hours, but it can go up to sixteen hours during the crawfish season." While the season for farm-raised crawfish begins in late January, the wild crawfish season does not begin until the spring when heavy rains fill the rivers.

Robin asserts that southern Louisiana produces the best crawfish in the world. Agreeing, Huval reasons that the clay soils of the bayous and numerous ponds provide the crawfish with a safe environment. During the often blistering dry season, crawfish seek moisture and bury themselves into the mud where they fall into semihibernation. "When the crawfish digs a hole in sandy soil to crawl into, the sand will fall back on top of the crawfish, killing it. The clay soil of the bayou won't collapse against the animal," Huval explains. As such, they survive to reach a larger size and develop greater quantities of meat.

Near the end of June, after heavy rainfall, Robin siphons the rain and river waters from his ponds in order to accommodate the growth of alligator grass, the staple of the crawfish's diet, and to lower the number of predators. However, Robin refuses to feed the crawfish that live in either the ponds or rivers. He intervenes only during harvest when he places a high-protein bait into a trap to attract the crawfish.

Wandering through The Fisherman's Wharf, Robin admits that he would retire tomorrow if he could. Smiling, he knows that he wouldn't do that because no one else but he, the Cajun, would really know how to take care of the small crawfish in the same way.

To clean up crawfish, let them soak in heavily salted water for fifteen minutes. Then, rinse them with cold water before cooking. This not only gives them a nice flavor, but it also gets rid of the muddy taste that crawfish sometimes bear.

RENÉ BAJEUX

Growing mussels

Despite the cold air blowing through Penn Cove Bay on Whidbey Island, Washington, a group of mussel farmers lean from their rocking boat, dip their hands into the water, and pull long ropes of black seed mussels from rafts floating in the waves. They swiftly pack the juvenile shellfish into long, netted tubes before plunging their gloved hands back into the sea to retrieve more. Eyeing the men closely, ducks float nearby on the rolling waves and wait for the opportunity to lunge at one of the shimmering shells. Meanwhile, an eagle soars overhead, gaining momentum to dive and catch one of the ducks in its claws, if not a salmon swimming just below the water's surface. Against the backdrop of the towering Cascade Mountains, nature plays in perfect balance and yields from her cobalt waters some of the most superb mussels in the world.

Ian Jefferds, manager of his family's mussel business, Penn Cove Shellfish, makes it clear that the bay's milieu goes far beyond beauty and underscores its technical attributes. As the portal to the Skagit and Stilla-guamish Rivers, the bay teems with nutrients released by the waterways, specifically plankton—the mussels' central diet. With an average temperature of 52°, the water is highly oxygenated and allows the shellfish "to respire in the water," explains Jefferds. This capacity, as well as an abundance of food, "provides the mussels with a sweeter, smoother flavor."

Despite the wealth of marine life, the original white settlers of Penn Cove Bay did not derive their food from the sea. When Coupeville, the small town resting by Penn Cove Bay, was founded in 1852, "people brought their habits and customs, which had nothing to do with seafood—they were 'meat and potatoes' people," Jefferds says, his hands extended in the air. "Who was thinking about shellfish? Not a damn one of them!"

The inhabitants soon discovered the bounty of the surrounding waters and began to harvest the sea with vigor. Within little time, the local North Pacific wild salmon became one of the most widely consumed fish in the country. Yet, even after a century of intensive fishing, mussels were not part of the local harvest.

In the mid-1970s, Jefferds's father, after retiring from the United States Army, decided to farm mussels in Penn Cove Bay. "My father realized that nobody was farming mussels," Jefferds remembers. "We had lived overseas in Europe and Asia where the mussel is a huge commodity, so we thought that there was a good opportunity here."

When the family initially started farming and selling mussels, however, "people thought we were selling bait," Jefferds remembers in a beguiled sort of way. Only after a local French chef began to promote the mussel as a delicacy in his restaurant and a series of newspaper articles featured mussels as something other than bait, did the Jefferdses succeed in changing the local mentality.

Despite the cold air blowing through Penn Cove Bay on Whidbey Island, Washington, a group of mussel farmers lean from their rocking boat, dip their hands into the water, and pull long ropes of black seed mussels from rafts floating in the waves. They swiftly pack the juvenile shellfish into long, netted tubes before plunging their gloved hands back into the ocean to retrieve more.

Jefferds sits in his office situated on a wooden deck on the bay. Rocking slowly in his seat, like a boat atop gentle waves, Jefferds looks out over his panoramic view and points to the cluster of 40 rafts where the mussels develop. In slow, articulate speech, he describes the growing process of the mussel known as "suspended culture."

"Beginning in May, mussels spawn and release their eggs into the water," Jefferds explains. Within twenty-four hours, each fertilized egg changes into a free-swimming larva. In the ensuing three weeks, the microscopic larva will develop a shell and attach itself, using a cementlike adhesive secretion, to a collector line—a rope hung from the rafts. Once secured, the mussels feed on the Cove's rich supply of plankton. Within days, thousands of small black shells can been seen hanging from the rafts into the ocean depths.

Once they have grown approximately one-half of an inch, the mussels are picked from the collector line and placed into a plastic, netted tube known as the mussel sock. By thinning the mussels from the collector line, the shellfish "grow more quickly to a uniform size," Jefferds says. The mussels then rest underwater in the sock for a year and are harvested once they reach a mature size of two and one-half to three inches. Suspended culture is widely practiced in Spain, France, Italy, and Scotland because it preserves the natural state of the mussel while allowing the animal to absorb the sea's myriad flavors. Although other harvesting methods are used, such as dredging -- where mussels are dragged from the ocean floor -- Jefferds warns that those practices "risk damage and trauma" to the animal.

Taking advantage of the salinity of the Bay's water, slightly diluted by the freshwater coming from the rivers' mouths, Jefferds has also begun to raise the Mediterranean mussel. The growth potential of this European variety can exceed that of the Penn Cove mussel by nearly two times. Yet, to cultivate the European crop, Jefferds must contend with the cold North Atlantic waters which often prevent the mussel from spawning. To deal with the problem, Jeffreds keeps the Mediterranean mussel breeders in a warmer hatchery until the larvae have morphed into microscopic mussel form and are ready to attach onto a collector line. Then, "they just do quite well" in the Bay's waters.

Jefferds is careful to point out that he has no favorite between the Penn Cove mussel and the Mediterranean, commenting simply that "they are different." Comparisons are futile in any event, since both are velvety representations of Penn Cove Bay's natural bounty.

Immerse the mussels in water and stir them up a bit to thoroughly cleanse them. Then cook the mussels quickly in a boiling white wine preparation of scallion, saffron, and chopped thyme. Afterwards, sautée them for 30 seconds; as soon as the shells open, they are ready.

THIERRY RAUTUREAU

Down in Key Largo: stone crab and spiny lobster

Among the hidden treasures surrounding the shipwrecked boats in the deep waters of the Florida Keys, two American bounties of a different sort can be discovered in live, vibrant color—the stone crab and the spiny lobster.

Although abundant in the water, there is little chance that anyone will actually see a full stone crab on a plate. Of the animal's famous pair of black-and-white snapping claws, only the larger one can be harvested, explains Tommy Hill, who, along with his family, has been harvesting crab claws for nearly thirty years. Unlike most shellfish, the stone crab has the capacity to regenerate a claw that has been lost or removed. Inhabiting deep holes and rocks along the Keys' coastline and Florida's west coast, the crab is accustomed to such incapacitation since constant scrimmages with hungry predators often result in a lost appendage. According to Hill, a claw will regenerate in approximately eighteen months, a process that could happen at least four times in a crab's life.

This specific feature of the crab, "doesn't stop it from eating," says Hill in good humor. Between May and October, the harvesting months, boats leave Key Largo every morning and head for the grassy, sandy ocean bottoms where crabs indulge in ample food. Fishermen use traps filled with fish heads and, in some cases, lobster meat. Once the traps are pulled onto the boat, the fishermen delicately remove a claw directly at the joint, careful to protect the animal from injury, then return the crab to the sea. Living in depths from 20 to 30 feet, the stone crab offers a sweet, firm meat which closely resembles lobster in taste and appearance.

Another delicacy from the emerald Florida Keys' waters, the spiny lobster -- also known as the Florida lobster -- is a distinct breed from its Maine cousin. A series of unique spines, two large antennae, and an absence of claws characterize the shellfish. "Like the stone and the blue crabs, the spiny and the Maine lobsters are two separate animals," Hill explains while holding up two specimens of a dark greenish brown color. "The Florida lobsters have a different texture and taste," which Hill describes as hardy yet sweet.

With a diet of fish, clams, seaweed, and conch, the spiny lobster absorbs the finest flavors of deeper dwelling animals and plant life. Their habit of roaming in depths between eight and 300 feet, however, can make them difficult to catch. "It's a skill that takes many years to learn," explains Tommy Hill (left), who has distributed seafood from Key Largo, Florida, for years. Hill also catches the stone crab. Only the claws of this shellfish, which regenerate, can be harvested.

With a diet of fish, clams, seaweed, and conch, the spiny lobster absorbs the finest flavors of deeper dwelling animals and plant life. Their habit of roaming in depths between eight and 300 feet, however, can make them difficult to catch. "It's a skill that takes many years to learn," Hill admits.

"You have to know when to put the traps, when to bait, and when to pull them out according to the time of the month."

Thanks to Hill and others like him, however, most food connoisseurs need only the skill of cracking a freshly steamed spiny lobster tail to discover one of Key Largo's richest treasures.

"Roast the whole spiny lobster in a very hot oven and let it rest for ten minutes. Cut it in half and add semi-salted soft butter, whipped with lemon and a few diced basil leaves."

ALAIN DUCASSE

Running free

Legendary for its rich meat and voluptuous pink-lipped shell, the conch was originally found in the waters extending from the Florida Keys down to Venezuela. Over time, however, the gastropod, known as *Strombus gigas*, or giant shell, was severely overharvested. Today, having nearly vanished from Florida waters, it dwells only off the coastlines of Belize, Jamaica, the Bahamas, and the Turks and Caicos Islands.

One American, however, has succeeded in farm-raising conchs on his small enclave in the Turks and Caicos Islands. Chuck Hesse currently harvests more than one million of the shellfish each year, providing a strong supply to American restaurants while lessening the strain on wild populations. He raises conch of different sizes and harvests unique variations of the thick, firm meat. Whether of a small or larger variety, conch meat has a tender interior and crisp exterior that release a soft but "crunchy" sensation when bitten into.

"The experience has been like *Alice in Wonderland*. Every day is a delight to live, a challenge," Hesse says. With his white Hemingway beard and expressive face, he explains that the conch lives a clandestine life, inhabiting shallow waters only after maturing and developing a full shell. With little written material on the subject, the first stages of a conch's life have remained a mystery.

Perhaps these enigmatic qualities explain the conch's mystical appeal. A story still stands in the Turks and Caicos that men on Christopher Columbus's expedition recovered a conch "as large as a calf's head." And although conch is harvested mainly for its meat, notably high in protein, the colorful, intricately designed shell is also used to make musical horns, knives, and decorative bowls. As fate would have it, however, Hesse quite unexpectedly landed on the islands and began to debunk the secrets of the conch.

"I've been 'running free,'" says Hesse about his life in the Caribbean, alluding to the sailing term that describes a boat's motion when wind rushes behind an extended sail. "You go so fast," he exalts with a swing of his arm, "but you don't feel it because you're going with the wind." A sigh escapes and his face sobers, "make one mistake, though, and the boom can flip you over."

Indeed, Hesse has been running free since arriving in the Turks and Caicos. After graduating from the United States Naval Academy in Annapolis, Maryland, in 1973, he changed fields to obtain a master's degree in marine biology. Focusing on the sea, he devised a plan to sail around the world and built a mahogany sloop named *Alondra*. He and his wife left from New England and set sail for the Virgin Islands, where Hesse's wife planned to begin her studies on conch growth. After a few months' travel, however, Hesse became intensely seasick and when a storm brewed, his wife put her foot down.

Colored by the moon, shaped by the primal geometry, it is the original dreamboat, the sacred submarine that carries fertility to its rendezvous with poetry. In his novel *Skinny Legs and All*, Tom Robbins perfectly describes the secretive conch. It is a mystical animal and one that almost disappeared from the Caribbean and Florida waters. Luckily, an American conceived of the idea to establish a conch farm in the Turks and Caicos islands, where he succeeded in raising the beautiful shellfish. On the sea farm, Georgia Williams (left) loves to play with a pet conch.

"Your judgment has become questionable," Hesse recalls her saying as she demanded that they rest at the first island they encountered. Landing on the island of South Caicos, they docked at a fishing village that supported a sparse population of 2,000 native and six nonnative people. Overwhelmed by the number of conch in the blue green island waters, the couple decided to conduct their studies there.

The Turks and Caicos' waters, "with a high concentration of calcium, and warmer temperatures," are the perfect environment for the shellfish. In a deep, gravelly voice, Hesse explains that "these two factors combined make it a lot easier for the conchs to build their shells, assuring their survival."

A gastropod snail, the conch is a close relative of the abalone and a distant relative of the scallop, oyster, and clam. Despite its simple nervous system, it can see through two large unblinking eyes surrounded by white lacey irises. When shadows arise, the conch will stealthily withdraw into its shell. It uses a foot, a sort of thick claw, to slowly navigate the bottom of the sea, although conch have been known to leap without warning. After observing the animal closely, Hesse noted that that the conch grazes on grass "like a sheep or a cow would." It occurred to him that it would be the ideal sea animal to raise, as one would raise livestock on land.

While Hesse jokingly refers to himself as a "conch cowboy," his primary interest is protecting the environment. Once accepted by the natives or "belongers," he began advocating for heightened protection of the area's remarkable marine life. His efforts were well-timed. Tourism and development had increased significantly, and the population on Providenciales, the central island of eight, expanded to 19,000. Chains of luxurious hotels and an international airport opened to accommodate the influx of visitors.

In order to assist the natives of the Turks and Caicos to preserve the environment, Hesse launched a nonprofit organization called PRIDE, the Protection of Reefs and Islands from Degradation and Exploitation. Through PRIDE's help, the Turks and Caicos have successfully created a body of 33 natural parks, reserves, and marine sanctuaries. Today, snorklers may catch a glimpse of a large sea turtle, stingrays, or parrot fish swimming just feet away from the shore.

What Hesse considers his greatest accomplishment, however, is the harvesting method he developed for conch. Purchasing a plot of beach property in Providenciales, Hesse built a complex of simple buildings, erected fenced "pastures" in the water, and began to raise conch from the earliest larval stage to maturity.

Today, Hesse keeps 200 male and female conch in his fenced pastures. Upon mating, a female conch can lay up to eight egg masses, each of which contains approximately 500,000 larvae (only one of which would likely survive to reach adulthood in the wild). Nicky Sanford-Handfield, one of the numerous native workers at the farm, collects the newly laid masses and brings them to the hatchery.

Hesse and his staff then confront the task of inducing the larvae to metamorphose. "That requires a chemical environment in the water for the conch. It morphs only when it senses something safe in the ocean," Hesse explains. When he started the farm, Hesse reviewed academic research reports and noted that this reaction occurred when conchs were introduced to a microalgae known as laurencia.

Therefore, after the thousands of larvae, each smaller than a pinhead, are initially placed in growing tanks for three weeks, they are then exposed to laurencia-filled waters for several hours. The laurencia induces the larvae to metamorphose into free-swimming veligers, or baby conch. About 70 percent of the larvae in the tanks grow too slowly for harvesting purposes and are returned to the ocean near the conch farm as a step in rebuilding the wild conch's population.

Hesse discovered, however, that the most difficult aspect in devising a successful harvesting process was knowing how to handle the conch after metamorphosis. Although it seemed less complicated to raise the conch once their shells had developed, Hesse quickly learned otherwise.

As he painfully recounts, Hesse made the mistake of placing 300,000 young conch into a fenced 60-acre ocean pasture. Believing that the porcupine fish, also swimming in the pastures, were harmless to the baby conch, he unknowingly "fenced the fox into the hen house." After a few months, 90 percent of his conch had disappeared. One staff member opened a fish's belly and found 13 little conch fillets inside.

All the wiser, Hesse now keeps the young conch in an enclosed farm building. They are placed in special trays filled with the high-calcium sand, necessary for shell growth, and immersed in water at the ideal temperature of 82°.

Once the conchs have achieved a size of two-thirds of an inch, they are transferred to onshore nursery ponds, each 50 feet in diameter, in which Hesse has re-created the circular motions of the ocean's tides. Nearly 1.5 million conchs are kept in the 42 ponds before they are moved to grazing sea pastures in the ocean. Ponds, like the trays, protect the young animals from their numerous predators, such as the stingray, lobster, crab, and the nurse shark. The octopus, which drills a hole in the shell, injects a paralyzing venom, and pulls the conch out, poses the greatest danger.

As conchs sexually mature, they develop the famous lip or curl on the side of their shells. After watching his first group of conch grow, Hesse realized that the animal matured at a slower rate than previously thought. For economic purposes, he decided to sample a 3-inch, twelve-month-old juvenile. He boiled it for a few seconds in salted water and tasted it. The flavor was tender and rich. He, therefore, created a new product, the ocean escargot. He also began to sell the 4-inch conch, naming it the Island Princess. Eventually, top American chefs, pleased with Hesse's selection, demanded an even larger conch. In response, Hesse cultivated the Pacific Rim Model, which tastes similar to the Island Princess but, since it matures at a slower rate, offers 20 percent more meat.

For the final growing stage, conchs are moved to a subsea (underwater) pasture, a 60-acre fenced portion of the Caicos Bank adjacent to the farm. There, over the course of two years, they absorb the rich flavors of the ocean and grow from three inches to adulthood.

Before the luxuriant conch meat can be savored, however, the animal must be extracted from the scroll-shaped shell. The traditional practice is to strike one shell against another directly on the apex, where the strong connecting muscle is located. Then, with the motion of a corkscrew, the muscle is slowly pulled from

the shell, drawing the animal out from behind. To this day, belongers still go to the sea, equipped with nothing more than a lemon, and spend an afternoon eating conch.

Hesse would love to spend all of his days sitting on the dock eating freshly caught conch and sharing lemons with the belongers. Involving the native population in his business has not only proved extraordinarily successful, but it has fostered many strong friendships.

But at this moment, Hesse sits working in his small office filled with books, documents, and a collection of conch shells. He cannot resist quoting Tom Robbins's words on conch in the novel, *Skinny Legs and All:*

"Colored by the moon, shaped by the primal geometry, it is the original dreamboat, the sacred submarine that carries fertility to its rendezvous with poetry."

And, as a sign of the past or a symbol of the future, *Alondra*, Hesse's mahogany boat, still stands in the middle of his tropical farm.

"Cook the ocean escargot (baby conch) very quickly so that they remain tender and toss them with fresh lime – but not so much that you mask their unique and subtle flavor."

RICHARD BENUSSI

SNAILS

The escargot's diet

Imagine a plate of the freshest fruits and vegetables -- leafy green spinach, carrots, and sliced apples -- presented raw without sauce or decoration. Fine dining in an upscale restaurant, perhaps, but it is also the five-star daily menu for the snails raised by Eddie Chupek on his Maryland farm.

Snails eat everything they like, but their taste can be finicky. Considered crop pests in farms and household gardens, the snails have the innate ability to find the best, most delicate vegetation. This high-maintenance diet astonished Chupek when, upon quitting his construction job in 1997 due to back injuries, he began to raise the small gastropod.

His wife suggested beginning a snail farm after she had watched a television program on escargot. "I first laughed at the idea," says Chupek. Yet the joke turned into a successful business, and through his company, US Snails, Chupek now raises hundreds of the French *petit gris* (little grays), also known as the California brown garden snail, per year. "It tastes just like mushroom meat!" Chupek exclaims while cooking dozens of the snails in a typical preparation of butter, garlic, and red wine.

Chupek's snails live in large, plastic barrels where they spend their lives eating and breeding. Indeed, snails are almost as well known for their bizarre sex life as for their prime meat. Hermaphrodites, both male and female in anatomy, snails mate slowly by projecting small spikes from their heads into their partner's head. Following six hours of connection, they detach and go their separate ways to each lay 100 eggs. Chupek encourages proper mating by placing small pans of dirt inside the barrels where the snails can easily lay their eggs.

Once Chupek decided to raise escargot, and submitted to satisfying their gastronomic demands, his job became quite easy. After he feeds the snails and cleans their containers, his only chore is to keep the slow-moving creatures moist and protected them from the heat with regular mists of water. At four months, the snails are ready to be blanched in boiling water with fresh lemon juice. Just before harvesting, Chupek feeds the snails basil for purging purposes, as well as to create a nicer flavor.

Although Chupek would love to send his escargot to restaurants live, such efforts have been legally banned to prevent the slippery animals from escaping and wreaking havoc on neighboring crops. Instead, Chupek delivers the snails as fresh as possible, just slightly cooked to kill bacteria. That way, chefs are free to prepare them in any succulent manner they wish—perhaps served over the same bed of fresh lettuce and fruits that snails find so irresistable.

"I love snails prepared Tampura-style, served with a Remoulade sauce with lots of lemon juice and fresh tips of fennel."

SANDRO GAMBA

SWEETS

Chocolate refined

In a factory not far from San Francisco, two men have mastered a symphony of chocolate. With instruments such as cocoa beans from Venezuela, Ghana, Trinidad, Madagascar, and Java, a virtual masterpiece of the nut-brown confection is played out.

John Scharffenberger and Robert Steinberg began to manufacture chocolate from bean to bar in 1997. Scharffenberger, a former sparkling-wine producer, had tired of marketing only champagne and sought more creative ways to manufacture food. Steinberg, a physician, had begun a hobby of culinary studies. Collecting their creative and scientific energies, the men conceived the idea of producing small quantities of a highly refined chocolate.

Dark, with a sharp bite, pure chocolate bearing the natural flavor of the cocoa bean stands far above the ubiquitous candy bar. Creating the sable delicacy from only sugar, vanilla beans, lecithin (an emulsifier), and cocoa beans, while carefully retaining the potency of cocoa flavor, has proven to be an experiment in science.

"The more books I read about chocolate, the more I realized that there were a variety of production methods, and very few manufacturers who were willing to release their secrets," Steinberg says.

Not that either of the men is willing to unveil their exacting touch. Unless that secret could be considered a constant search for the best cocoa bean and an ideal balance of flavor, which Steinberg calls, "a basic chocolate flavor and fruitiness with an acidity so that at the end you're left with a long finish and a clean sensation in your mouth."

The chocolatiers begin their work by hand-selecting the best cocoa beans from jungle forests. Traveling as far away as Honduras and Venezuela, the men visit planters who grow, on average, no more than ten acres of cocoa. Due to the small plots of land, any given region will yield varying qualities of beans. As such, Steinberg and Sharffenberger travel widely to find the best beans of the year. "In a single bag of beans, there might be the work of hundreds of farmers."

Back home, in their small factory where vintage equipment contrasts with the surrounding industrial neighborhood, beans are sorted and tasted. Each variety produces differing amounts of sugar, moisture, and acidity which, in combination, dictate different cooking times. The husked bean, broken into small roasted pieces, called nibs, becomes the very essence of the chocolate.

"The beans have a tremendous amount of complexity of flavor," explains Steinberg, while nibbling on a chocolate square. Part of his secret is an expansive collection of those bean flavors, "red fruit flavors, tropical or spicy tastes, flavors that have a slight cheese quality, hints of tobacco or toasted nut flavors."

The nibs are placed into a granite-based machine and ground into a paste-like substance by two attached granite rollers. In crushing the nibs, cocoa butter is released as the fibrous walls surrounding the pieces of the bean are broken down. Crystal sugarcane and whole vanilla beans from Tahiti and Madagascar are then added to the mix.

Steinberg calculates many of the technical aspects of chocolate making. Scribbling on a piece of paper, he explains the scientific mystery of chocolate. A product with 70 percent chocolate means that 29 percent is added sugar and one percent is vanilla and lecithin. The 70 percent chocolate component is part cocoa solid (the distilled bean) and part cocoa butter (the fat). As such, the content of the chocolate is based less on sugar and more on the amount of pure cocoa solid. Together, cocoa solids and cocoa butter are known as chocolate liquor or, in French, *Pâte de Cacao*. In the end, the consumer just knows the taste is beyond compare.

Sweet, bittersweet and dark chocolate varieties bear fruity and nutty aromas. As Scharffenberger puts it, they might be likened to a concerto. Steinberg, on the other hand, equates them to chamber music—while a connoisseur distinguishes each instrument's contribution, an amateur, who hears only the set and not the individual notes, still appreciates the overall experience.

"A slice of bread, very cold butter, and chocolate on the top - let's bite into it! Adults are ashamed to love it and children adore it with joy."

LAURENT MANRIQUE

Cold treats

Fresh ice creams and sorbets, served either as a *trou normand* to cleanse the palate or as dessert, add the divine breath to any meal. Available in almost every conceivable flavor, they represent nearly all the flora, fruit, and tree blossoms that nature produces.

At Egg Farm Dairy in Peekskill, New York, Jonathan White has made it his mission to raise the ice cream and sorbet experience to a higher, richer level. Ironically, his method to achieve such a feat is simple. He uses only milk, cream, honey, pure cane sugar, fresh fruits, ginger, chocolate, and maple syrup in his creations. He adamantly refuses to add any gums, stabilizers, or preservatives to the products. White dismisses, as inconsequential, the fact that to have such fresh, overwhelming flavors the shelf life of his ice cream is less than eight weeks.

White, who confesses that he makes what he likes, says that part of his secret is the freshness of his ingredients. From the ginger roots he buys, White himself extracts a liquid essence that he makes into syrup. He immediately adds sugar and finishes the ice cream. The flavor, White says, "starts gradually and builds up to a crescendo in just about the time it takes to say 'fresh ginger.'" In addition to the all-time-favorite chocolate variety, some flavors, including maple syrup, strawberry-rhubarb, and grapefruit (made from Florida juice), are seasonal.

Thus, the biggest challenge for a consumer is not to refrain from indulging, but to select the best among all these treats. White has an answer for those struggling to decide which flavor to sample: "Try everything."

"Eat a lot, a lot, a lot! At the right temperatures, it starts to melt on the sides and is very soft."

ALAIN DUCASSE

VEGETABLES

Four seasons in the garden

In front of the farm at Chef's Garden, yards away from Lake Erie, an old tractor with a spindly steering wheel and elongated 1930s front engine stands in strong bearing of the past. As the twenty-first century begins, guaranteeing new power-enhancing machinery, a handful of farmers claim the tractor as a mascot against technological dominance.

On their 75-acre farm of greens and vegetables in Huron, Ohio, brothers Lee and Bob Jones are two such farmers. They apply a philosophy that most modern farmers don't, by working the soil without advanced engines, fertilizers, or chemicals. Reading through the old books that their father, who launched the Ohio farm in 1961, keeps in his cluttered office, the brothers taught themselves how to grow vegetables according to season and traditional farming methods.

"It's not always the yield that is the most important," declares Lee, the older of the two brothers. "It's the variety and the handling of the product and the soil."

Their motto is to grow vegetables slowly and gently, in full accord with nature. All that a farmer can add is special care applied through knowledge of the plants.

"My father has a saying that he's been telling me for years," says Bob: "The best fertilizer that the farmer can put on comes from the bottom of his shoes." Bob, who studied agriculture in college, confesses that it took him five years to understand his father's maxim. Today, the meaning is clear. "The best thing a farmer can do for his crop is to continually walk the field and look at the plants. Walk, walk, and walk, and watch them grow to see what's happening."

The harvesting season starts with the spring season, and in this part of Ohio, that means asparagus. "The first thing we look for is asparagus poking out through the ground," explains Bob. "That's a sign that the soil temperature is warming and vegetables are growing." Typically green, if asparagus is grown without light, thereby suspending the chlorophyll process, it will become snow-white and develop a softer, more tender texture (the Joneses grow this variety as well).

Rhubarb and spinach soon follow the asparagus. Due to the warmer temperatures that the lake creates on the farm, the Joneses "over winter" the spinach. Bob elaborates, "planted back in September, the spinach crop eventually receives a good blanket of snow to protect it from the coldest months of December and

208

January." Lake Erie, Lee joins in, does the rest. "The large body of water warms up in the summer to 70°, and as we're going into the fall season, the lake will hold us from getting too cold."

To harvest earlier crops of spinach, the Joneses grow a juvenile variety indoors. The small leaves develop a more potent flavor. Another baby vegetable the Joneses harvest prior to spring's advance is a bright red radish known as the *Radish d'Avignon*. Also grown indoors for a longer season, the mild and sweet vegetable is called the breakfast radish by the French.

The Joneses have become familiar with baby vegetables in order to serve their special clients, some of the most demanding chefs in the country. This relationship stems from a challenge posed to the Jones brothers in the 1980s when they were selling vegetables at the Cleveland farmer's market.

A few years after recovering from a bad storm that destroyed most of the farm, Lee took a retail stand at the farmer's market and began to sell freshly harvested vegetables from his truck. One day, Iris Bailin, a chef from Cleveland, stopped to look at the vegetables and asked for a small zucchini which still had the blossom attached to its tip. Back at the farm, Lee discussed the request with his father, the resident vegetable expert. Puzzled, his father responded, "well, these people in Cleveland are on drugs. Forget about her, she'll never be back."

But Bailin did come back, Wednesday after Wednesday, repeatedly inquiring about her flower-stemmed zucchini. Finally, prompted by interest, Lee picked a vegetable the size the woman had described and presented it to her from his stand. "I shocked her," Lee says. "She started screaming in the middle of the market, 'Oh my God, that's just like I saw in Paris! I've got to introduce you to my friends the chefs.'"

From there, Lee and his brother were pulled into the restaurant business and eventually made it their primary business. They expanded the farm's fields to grow 45 varieties of zucchini and developed a class of zucchini, much to Bailin's delight, that holds its flower even after being steamed.

"What we're doing is counterculture to today's mass-produced agriculture," explains Bob. The brothers worry only about the flavor, the color, and the shape of the vegetable. "Chefs are the artists, we provide them with the paints," asserts Lee. Indeed, their palate holds a lot of color. Carrots are long and ball shaped, or white with a milder flavor. Turnips and radishes wrap up the spring and open the summer. Squash, tomatoes and peppers develop brilliant ruby colors that match the sunset's spectrum. Eggplants, grown in 30 different varieties, range from the small golf-ball sized specimens to the green, the purple and the marbled ones.

Almost all the vegetables the Joneses grow have a miniaturized counterpart. More work is involved with the petite varieties to keep all the flavors and nutrients intact. "It's virtually an impossible task," explains Bob. A task that took "years and years of experiments," echoes Lee.

Among the baby vegetables and lettuces the Joneses produce are the purple Brussels sprouts. A fall vegetable, the small flush-colored sprouts were the product of research the brothers conducted in the early 1990s. Smaller than the green variety, but a hint stronger, the little round vegetable looks like a dried flower. "It lends itself to creativity on the plate," Bob comments.

Brussels sprouts (top left), peas (bottom left), breakfast radishes, carrots, eggplants, tomatoes, zucchinis, and asparagus— almost every kind of vegetable grows at the Chef's Garden in Ohio. Lee Jones (right) and his family farm seventy-five acres of land with care and love, respecting the seasons and leaving the soil to do its work. "The best fertilizer that the farmer can put on comes from the bottom of his shoes," the Joneses explain.

While most vegetables become dormant during the winter, watermelon, red-meat radishes, black radishes, salsifi (also called the oyster plant), and the heavier root vegetables, such as rutabaga, flourish in the cooler parts of the year. At the turn of the last century, people stored winter vegetables in root cellars where the temperature remained an ideal 56°. But "nobody has a root cellar anymore," Lee says a bit wistfully.

Times have changed, as have farming techniques. Lee tells the story of a woman, not so long ago, who stopped by the farm and stared at a potato digger. The machine turned the potatoes from the ground, shook the dirt, and gently placed the vegetable back down on the ground. The potato was then picked up by hand. The woman, amazed at the antiquity of the machine, wanted to take it to the Thomas Edison Birthplace Museum a few miles away from the farm.

"Wait a minute," Lee told her, "we're still using it."

"With its natural sweet flavor and bright red color, the Breakfast Radish makes a great garnish."

JOHN D'AMICO

Lilliputian lettuces

It can be semantically confusing. One would imagine that "baby" lettuce would be the smallest member of the lettuce family, and that the "petite" lettuce would be the next step up. To the contrary. While baby lettuce can grow up to five inches long, the petite lettuce will be harvested before reaching three inches. The truth is, both derive from the same plant, but with pronounced differences that result from the demands of upscale chefs and the eccentricity of one family.

Brothers Lee and Bob Jones have grown baby lettuces at the Chef's Garden in Huron, Ohio, since the early 1980s. Both men attribute a large part of their success to Lake Erie, which, located near the farm, provides the perfect environment to cultivate the plants. According to Lee, under the cool breeze that lifts off the lake in the fall, the plants build a certain resistance to brisk night temperatures. Without this adaptation, the lettuces "would be frozen completely, like dried leaves in the morning and crumble if harvested," Lee asserts. By allowing the lettuces to spawn slowly in the fall air, they become crisp in texture and brilliant in color.

Although they are all varieties of "babies," the lettuces harvested at a mature six to ten weeks range in color, shape, and piquancy. The Red Oak, with leaves shaped like those of its namesake tree, darkens to a red color in the spring and fall and bears a sweet taste. Also scarlet colored, the small leaf of the Lolla Rossa mischievously curls like a cherub's forelock. The Speckle, appropriately named, looks as though dappled with red paint.

The younger petite lettuces, harvested before the typical growing period of six to ten weeks, are a rare treat. "Most of the growers would not harvest them earlier because the yield wouldn't be there," explains Bob who, after creating the baby lettuces, became inspired to produce a younger, smaller variety.

To achieve the petites' rare flavors and textures, Bob grows the lettuces slowly, allowing the plants to develop a good body despite their size. "It's harvested so young that it's just the ultimate in tenderness," Lee says. As Bob describes it, the taste of the petite variety is "a bit softer" than the baby lettuces.

Although the brothers grew their first petite lettuces in the early 1990s, they did not market them until chefs made specific requests for the product nearly six years later. Today, the demands are overwhelming.

The idea of a "microlettuce" decorating haute cuisine in the near future is not so far-fetched. Sure enough, the plants will be another diminutive Jones creation.

"Simply toss your custom blend of petite lettuces in aged balsamic vinegar, extra virgin oil, sea salt, and fresh ground pepper."

JEFFREY WEISS

Fingerling potatoes

Crescent shaped, curved like a half-moon, the fingerling potato's unique shape lends itself to poetic metaphor. Ed Alberti, who grows the potatoes in the Catskill Mountains of Upstate New York is more pragmatic, "it's shaped like your finger." Yet, don't be fooled, the man is passionate about his potatoes. Sitting next to his wife, Laurie, Alberti breaks into animated motion describing the seven different types of the two- to four-inch gourmet potato he cultivates.

"The Ozette is beige with a pale colored flesh. The French fingerling is red on the outside and has a red core. Then you have the Russian Banana, Austrian Crescent, La Ratte—all have yellow-fleshed interiors," he says listing his favorites. According to Alberti, the taste differences are subtle, ranging from earthy to nutty. "You just have to try them all."

Alberti waxes idyllic, "the fingerling business is different from the regular potato business. They serve a lot of these whole on the plate. When you are serving potatoes whole on the plate, they have got to be good potatoes."

To ensure a level of perfection, Alberti believes that everything must be done by hand once the potatoes have been turned from the ground by machine. At that point, crews of people pick the potatoes from the dirt and begin the inspection process. The potatoes are then transported in wooden crates to the warehouse where they are washed and inspected a second time. "Sorted every step of the way," potatoes are constantly rejected, or culled, rendering the grading "a never-ending process," says Alberti. Last year, before a crop of 200 tons of potatoes was yielded, nearly 50 percent had been culled. "You just have to sell the best potatoes, quality is everything," Alberti insists.

Constant inspection of the potato plant itself is required from the beginning. "You have to keep on monitoring all the fields for diseases and insects that might attack the potato plant." The plant's growth is also closely followed. "Potatoes are vines. After they get to be a couple of feet tall, they will start to bend over. The plants can get up to five feet long. Eye level! So you can't get an accurate idea of how big they are with a quick look."

Alberti's body of knowledge is impressive by any account, but particularly for a man who abandoned his life as a dairy farmer only three years ago to grow potatoes. "I was looking to get out of the milk business," Alberti wearily recalls, describing a market chronically plagued by decreasing prices.

In 1996, he began to look for alternative farming projects and contacted the New York City Watershed Project. Giant reserves in Upstate New York, known as the "Watershed Region" provide the metropolitan

area with some of the purest water in the country. To maintain the pristine quality of the water, the Watershed Project began a correlating agricultural program to encourage local farming. "Agriculture was a preferred land use," Alberti explains.

A program director from the project visited Alberti and suggested that, since top chefs had a demand for fingerlings, he should try cultivating them. Intrigued, Alberti attended seminars, conducted research, and learned how to structure a "specialty potato program." He planted five acres the first year, presented his product to upscale restaurants, and anxiously awaited the results.

"The response was great, overwhelming. We sold every potato that we grew."

Since then, Alberti has become the largest fingerling producer in the area. Last year, he expanded his farm to 30 acres and yielded 200 tons of potatoes. He was one of the first members of a potato cooperative initiated by the Watershed Project. Today, the cooperative is comprised of ten potato growers.

"The cooperative idea is appealing. It allows all of us to share the labor, our experiences, our equipment," Alberti, who is reportedly the only one to make his living exclusively from the potatoes, enthuses.

Alberti learned that the best planting ground is "a sandier loam, a lighter soil." As a result, last year he rented a larger tract of land with such soil in order to improve the quality of the potatoes and to enable quicker growth. "Now we pick out the best soil that we can find, even it it's not on our farm."

The planting process begins in April. The seed, a piece of potato bearing an eye or small indentation, is carefully selected from the previous year's crop or purchased from a state certifying agency. Dusted for protection, particularly against blight, the seeds are prepared for planting.

Alberti employs machines only for very specific purposes on the farm. A planter is used to dig furrows in the fields where the seeds are deposited and, later, to turn the potatoes for harvest. A hiller plows through the fields to cover the plants with dirt, "so that you have a mound, approximately six to eight inches high protruding from the ground, which is called a hill." Hilling provides the potato with a growing space. Without it, the potatoes "will pop out of the soil and turn green," Alberti warns. Once the plants reach eight inches, another hilling is done in which nearly half of the plant is covered to prevent sunburn.

Fortunately, with such intensive labor required to grow and harvest the small tuber, the shelf life is a "long time, given the right conditions." Harvested from September through November, the potatoes are sold until the end of June.

Alberti imagines himself continuing his work well into the future. While expansion is a possibility, he refuses to sacrifice quality. "You have to pick the potatoes up, then pick them up again, then handle them, handle them, handle them. You get on your hands and knees and crawl up through the field. Most people aren't going to do that." Alberti will, because, as he says smiling, "I do enjoy a good crop."

"I like the fingerling potatoes cooked in their skins in water with sea salt. I savor them plain or with butter and olive oil."

ALAIN DUCASSE

219

Ruby red tomatoes

The moon has set and dawn is trying to warm as Alan Marcelli begins to wander among tomato vines in Homestead, Florida. The January air, bearing a distinct chill, warns of an upcoming storm.

Despite his smile, Marcelli, president of the New York-based Lucky's Real Tomatoes, is fully aware that tomorrow the weather may cause him to lose good tomatoes. Calmly, he watches other men not so calmly pick green tomatoes in an effort to save as many as possible. Only the plain red ones interest Marcelli today. The nearly red ones, which Marcelli will pick tomorrow or the next day, are at the greatest risk of damage by the approaching cool front. But it is a risk he is willing to take—his twenty year reputation for providing only the best sun-ripened tomatoes is on the line.

"Everything that I ask a farmer to do goes against today's traditional farming," admits Marcelli. "I want them to keep the tomatoes even though there might be a storm."

Younger generations may not remember that tomatoes were not always available year round in the United States. Improved shipping has made ripe tomatoes more accessible to the public. Nonetheless, many tomatoes are still picked green and sent to mature in greenhouses, where much of the natural flavor is lost. Instead of relying on manmade ripening procedures, the Marcelli family insists on marketing only the freshest, crimson colored tomatoes that, as Marcelli describes, "explode" with natural flavor.

Among the rows of twisting tomato vines, Marcelli picks three specimens. Slicing the first, rather green, tomato in half, Marcelli points to a red spot on the top and inside. This one, he says, will be placed in a refrigerator and artificially matured for the market. He inspects the second tomato. Although red, the color is not sufficiently intense for Marcelli. The third one, round, tender and brilliantly red, but not too soft, is perfect. It will be picked as soon as it dries from the morning dew. Taken at its ripest and stored at 60 to 65°, the tomato will have a three- to six-day shelf life.

The Marcelli family works with tomato growers ranging from Homestead, Florida, up to the North Carolina mountains. "Farmers are an extension of the family," smiles Marcelli. Reciprocating the respect, growers know that Marcelli will pay top dollar for only the ripest tomatoes.

Marcelli admits that his buying methods will cost him not only expense but a lot of tomatoes, either through shipping or, simply, through time. Even when trucked to Marcelli's sister, Lucky Lee, the company's namesake, in their Brooklyn office, "we lose five to 30 percent of the vegetables," Lee says.

Unpredictable weather, however, poses the greatest threat. The weather in Homestead, sunny and dry nine months of the year, should not be a negative factor for farming. Yet, thousands of crops were destroyed by Hurricane Andrew in the early 1990s. Nonetheless, the land in Homestead remains expensive agricultural property.

"It is the southernmost spot for growing plants in the whole country," Marcelli says. There, he finds all the varieties he is looking for, from large beefsteak tomatoes to the smaller lantern-shaped yellow ones.

Holding a round, red specimen in his hand, Marcelli advises not to always look for external beauty. Sometimes the less esthetically pleasing tomatoes may very well be the most flavorful.

"Cut thick slices of tomatoes and then fry them with garlic butter."

ERIC RIPERT

223

Peppers and squash

Two farmers in Sonoma County, California, insist on maintaining a sense of humor. Brother and sister, Wayne and Lee James, who have been growing vegetables since 1980, recount a favorite paradox. In the same years that their pumpkin and squash crops have been abundant, their chili peppers have been prudent. And when the weather induces hundreds of peppers to sprout from their vines, the squash plants demure in modest growth to their fiery neighbors. "I don't know how we would ever handle a big chili and squash harvest in the same year," wrote Lee in a small newsletter to her regular customers, "but I'd like to try."

Lee is known as the "Chili Lady" at the San Francisco farmer's market, where she sells her vegetables every Saturday. Wayne and Lee started farming as soon as their parents bought land in Healdsburg, California. Wayne remembers those early days when a wooded, undisturbed area surrounded the property. Today, although three-hundred-year-old oak trees still stand, they are widely separated by fast-rising homes and, at night, they glow in waves of artificial light. The soil, nonetheless, remains perfect for farming.

In memory of the farm's original spirit, the brother-and-sister team have successfully resisted urban development and continued to grow as many vegetables as possible. Supporting themselves almost entirely, they raise ducks, chickens, and pigs for food and sheep for wool. Missing only a dairy cow, they buy their butter and milk from the local market.

With a limited number of crops, they count on a limited number of customers to purchase their products —primarily shoppers at the San Francisco farmer's market and a small collection of private clients.

The Jameses grow no fewer than 40 varieties of peppers, each a different shape, color, and flavor. Their fame, however, is derived from the hot and spicy peppers which, when bitten into, bring tears to the eyes. Their smoked and dried chilis, including the ancho, cascabel, guajillo, pasilla, and costeño, reflect the sun-kissed influence of Mexico and the American West. Each variety has been slowly dried outdoors in order to maintain the original potency, color and flavor.

Chipotle peppers, or "smoke chili" in the ancient Aztec tongue, range from mild to hot and are smoked for five days following their harvest at the peak of ripeness. After delicately sorting the peppers by hand, Wayne and Lee spread them on trays and place them into a smoker, fired by burning apple or pear wood. Coming from the smoker, which is used only for five months of the fall and winter seasons, the flavor bears the natural, rich spiciness and aroma of the chipotle, accented with a light smoky flavor.

Two farmers in Sonoma County, California, insist on maintaining a sense of humor. Brother and sister Wayne (left) and Lee (right) James, who have been growing vegetables since 1980, recount a favorite paradox. In the same years that their pumpkin and squash crops have been abundant, their chili peppers have been prudent. And when the weather induces hundreds of peppers to sprout from their vines, the squash plants demure in modest growth to their fiery neighbors.

226

Fresh peppers, however, also make their way into the market. Some are mellifluous and soft, such as the sweet cherry pepper, ideal for decoration with its delicate round shape, or the jingle bell, which is large enough to stuff with ground meat. Other peppers, although fresh, such as the aji, a Peruvian pepper notable for its pungent aroma, can set throats on fire.

When the weather is not overbearingly hot, winter squashes take over as the central crop. Cut into two pieces, the yellow spaghetti squash is easily recognizable by its marked resemblance to pasta noodles. Caramel-colored butternut squash, which has a deep red interior and smooth flavor, is often served with a touch of brown sugar. Adding flashes of brilliant fire-orange color to the gardens, the Jameses grow a plot of traditional pumpkins.

During the off-season in the late fall, Wayne and Lee cover the ground with a thick layer of green grass to enhance the soil's quality. The grass not only protects the soil from erosion, but its full array of nutrients enriches the ground, making it healthier for the next season's crops.

Although the multicolor squash and peppers normally splash the ground with a rainbow of deep harvesting colors, the grass cover marks a spot of emerald fertility in an area where farming has become as rare as the jewel it resembles.

"I like the small, strong and mild squashes roasted with olive oil and stuffed with ricotta, sea salt and pepper. They make a great appetizer."

SYLVAIN PORTAY

Small is beautiful

The Farm at the South Mountain in Phoenix, and its magnificent 12 acres of dry, Arizona soil, supports lush beds of vegetables and greens. The Eden-like farm embodies the philosophy "small is beautiful," coined by economist E. F. Schumacher and embraced by Wayne Smith, owner and founder of the farm. There is no coincidence that Schumacher's book is propped in the middle of Smith's office. "I call it my Bible," he says. The Farm at the South Mountain is the result of Smith's aspiration "to bring people to experiment with a gentler lifestyle."

A landscape architect-turned-farmer, Smith grows 100 varieties of seasonal vegetables and 60 different herbs. Tomatoes, cabbages, artichokes, spinach, snow peas, radishes, eggplants, garlic, and lavender top a seemingly endless list of leguminous products that can either constitute a meal or complement foods with crisp, natural flavor.

"When you eat good food, you feel better, you think better, you're more energetic and not sluggish," opines Smith who has, as part of his health philosophy, excluded all meat from his diet in order to pursue athletic activities.

The slim sixty-five-year-old farmer and restaurant director prides himself on having finished third in his age division in the 1983 Iron Man World Championship in Hawaii. When not farming, he spends most of his time biking, swimming, and running. It was while riding up to the mountains in the early 1980s that Smith first discovered the land where he would build his lifetime achievement. He fell in love with a row of picturesque fields which, although rather dilapidated, were crowned with pecan trees. Noticing a "For Sale" sign on a gate circling a house, he wheeled his bicycle up to the front door and knocked. When no one answered, he went to the back door and realized that the property, "full of debris," was not in prime condition. A voice finally barked out, "what the hell do you want?"

Answering Smith's inquiries, the owner, Skeeter Coverdale, a retired cattleman, snapped, "the farm goes from that fence to that one, and I want lots of money." Smith laughs now, "I had my helmet and my goggles on, and he was surely thinking, 'What is this dummy bothering me about?'"

Born in Florida, Smith had lived most of his childhood in Missouri. Finding the Midwest too "rigid" and "slow," he moved to Arizona in 1965. In the late 1960s, Smith launched a landscape architecture and land planning company. But that afternoon, standing on Coverdale's porch, Smith once again was changing his life's path.

When Coverdale failed to make a decision about whether or not to sell, Smith returned home and became consumed with ideas for the farm. He went to bed, only to wake at 3:00 A.M., gripped by a fear that

A landscape architect-turned-farmer, Wayne Smith (previous) grows 100 varieties of seasonal vegetables and sixty different herbs. Tomatoes, cabbages, artichokes, spinach, snow peas, radishes, eggplant, garlic, and lavender are just some of the products that can either constitute a meal or complement other foods with crisp, natural flavor. "When you eat good food, you feel better, you think better, you're more energetic and not sluggish," promises Smith.

someone else would purchase the property. "So I drove down to the gate and put a towel over the 'For Sale' sign," Smith remembers, amused at his panic. The following morning, he returned to the farm with a six-pack of beer for Coverdale, negotiated a deal, and bought The Farm at the South Mountain.

One of Smith's primary goals in purchasing the property was to demonstrate that a small 10' x 10' garden of vegetables could sustain a family of five for one year. To do so, he turned a section of his farm into a "learning" organic garden and, hiring chef Hallie Harron, opened a corresponding restaurant. "The whole project is Wayne's vision," Harron explains. "Before he planted his first carrot, he worked the land for five years."

Smith bases a large part of his success on the area's impressive irrigation system. "We have the Salt River Project, a wonderful series of lakes that was created after the local government dammed the river at the turn of the century." Flowing directly from the mountains, "the water is a little salty from its high mineral content." Originally, Smith had used the city's water through drip irrigation. When he discovered that the water was replete with chemicals, however, he switched to flood irrigation which releases only water from the lakes. Although Smith needed to slow production during the transition, the pristine water he tapped into, and now has available for his plants, made the effort worthwhile.

Another secret at The Farm at the South Mountain is the use of compost made from grass clippings. "We till it into the soil before we plant, and when the plants get tall enough, we use it as mulch to keep the soil cool and to hold in the moisture," explains Smith. The compost then turns the desert soil into a growing one. Harron says with spirit, "it's the best soil one can find in Arizona. For a brief moment of time, you're in a green, lush area."

Driving his golf cart across the garden, Smith points out a large Napalita cactus that bears a sweet fruit. "The pads that come out early in the summer are very tender." He stops the cart and holds a branchlike extension in his hand. "Brush off the stickers, and that's what's used for salsa." The wonderful thing about cactus, he adds, is that it will reproduce anywhere as soon as it's planted.

After passing by "Pete the Peacock," a colorful, free-roaming bird, Smith steps into a garden and inspects his elephant garlic, recognizable by its large, clumpy cloves referred to as "big claws," and his California white garlic, which he describes as "smaller and sweet."

Smith looks at the scarecrow standing guard over his botanical riches. "If somebody asked, 'did I plan all this,' I can't say that I have, it just unfolded."

Few cities grow as quickly as Phoenix, but at The Farm at the South Mountain, Smith has not only created a paradisiacal garden where time has stopped, but he has managed to show people how to appreciate and do the same.

"My favorite is soup made with Wayne Smith's green garlic, rich chicken stock, and local cream. With those three ingredients, I've discovered the world's best soup."

ALESSANDRO STRATTA

List of illustrations

Index by products

234

Index by names

Acknowledgments

Alain Ducasse and Jean-Christian Agid would like to express their special thanks and recognition to Patricia Gaviria and the amazing value of her work in creating *Harvesting Excellence*. Her dedication to the beautiful written word, as well as her culinary curiosity allowed this book to exist. Extraordinary thanks are also extended to Gwénaëlle Gueguen, whose daily presence and professional coordination led to the realization of this work, and to Axel Icard, a promising young photographer.

Although not officially sponsored, *Harvesting Excellence* would not have been possible without the efforts of Continental Airlines, particularly the staff of their Paris office -- Marie-Laure Gougeon and Ildut Marc -- who worked endless hours to find the best, seemingly impossible, flight connections.

We thank all the people who have made this book possible, starting with the bakers, cheese makers, farmers, fishermen, ranchers, and food distributors who not only gave us their time, but also remained available for additional comments. Although we are unable to name them all, our gratitude covers their efforts.

Alain Ducasse's discoveries stem in large part from the guidance of several top chefs in America, namely, René Bajeux, Sandro Gamba, Laurent Manrique, Jean-Louis Palladin, Sylvain Portay, Eric Ripert, and Alessandro Stratta, as well as food distributor Ariane Daguin.

A book is frustrating in its limits. While we would have loved to write stories on all the outstanding food producers in the United States, and there are dozens, space would not allow it. As such, it would be unfair to overlook: Jay Moon, Keith Smith, and Bill Burkhardt in Cape Canaveral, Florida, for their fresh calico scallops; the Odom family, who raise superior quail in South Carolina; Rick and Kristie Knoll, who produce figs in Stockton, California; Larry Jacobs, for his herbs and vegetables; and Greg Hinson, who has created a wonderful Meyer lemon olive oil in California.

Jean Christian Agid and Axel Icard are indebted to all the farmers, ranchers, fishermen, and distributors who generously shared their homes and faciletes. Among them, Jan Holder, Elisabeth Hughes, Linda-Marie Loeb, Lee Jones, and Patty Weihl welcomed us warmly. Gérard Agid (The Windsor Court Hotel, New Orleans), Ron Hauck (Westmark Hotel Sitka, Alaska) and all the people of Sitka, and Laurent Manrique (The Campton Place, San Francisco) greeted us with genuine kindness and graciousness, as did Philippe Delouvrier, the Shearer family, Bill and Wenke Sterns (in New York City), and Bernardo and Marilyn Gaviria (in Albany, New York).

238

Our appreciation goes to all the chefs and restaurants who invited us to sample their products and creations: René Bajeux at the *Windsor Court Hotel* in New Orleans, Louisiana; Richard Benussi at the *Barefoot Café* in the Turks and Caicos Islands; Laurent Carillon at *La Provence* in Orlando, Florida; David Grant at *l'Aubergine* in Portland, Maine; Hallie Harron at *The Farm at the South Mountain* in Phoenix, Arizona; Pat Huval at *The Fisherman's Wharf* in Louisiana; Alain Lecomte at the *Prince Michel* in Virginia; both Laurent Manrique at the *Campton Place* and Sylvain Portay at the *Ritz Carlton* in San Francisco, California; and Jean-Louis Palladin at *Palladin* in New York.

For the guided visits of the San Francisco farmer's market we acknowledge the assistance provided by Laurent Manrique and Ollivier Regenensi, as we do to René Bajeux for the visit of the New Orleans farmer's market.

Not only did Josh Ellsworth and Julia Gaviria give us a house in which to rest in Manhattan, but Julia also read each draft and provided invaluable editorial comments and suggestions. Margaret Braver provided excellent line editing guidance in rendering the final edition of the book, while Mathilde Dupuy d'Angeac's devotion and professionalism are visible on every page. Thanks are also extended to Vannina Maestracci-Calais.

In Paris, Danièle Granet, the executive director of the CFPJ (Center for Training Professional Journalists), understood the scope of the book and the time required to complete it by deadline. Her advice was of great value.

Jean-Christian Agid would like to forward his recognition to both Angela Haines and Melanie Huff, at New York University and Columbia University, respectively, who devoted themselves to teaching him how to write in English. His thoughts also go to Rhoda Lipton, Derwin Johnson, and Scotti Williston, his professors at the Graduate School of Journalism at Columbia University, and their unparalleled instruction during his studies there in 1997 and 1998. Their lessons followed him in every interview he made and every story he wrote.

Last but not least, Alain Ducasse wants to extend his personal gratitude to Jean-Christian Agid whose passion, enthusiasm, and inspiration led to the unique stories of those who harvest excellence.

The chefs tips were provided by:

RENÉ BAJEUX: The Windsor Court Hotel, New Orleans, Louisiana

RICHARD BENUSSI: Barefoot Café, Providenciales, Turks and Caicos Islands

JOHN D'AMICO: Chez François, Vermilion, Ohio

ALAIN DUCASSE: Alain Ducasse at the Essex House, Manhattan, New York

SANDRO GAMBA: Nomi, Chicago, Illinois

DAVID GRANT: L'Aubergine, Portland, Maine

HALLIE HARRON: The Farm at the South Mountain, Phoenix, Arizona

ALAIN LECOMTE: Prince Michel, Leon, Virginia

LAURENT MANRIQUE: Campton Place, San Francisco, California

JEAN-LOUIS PALLADIN: Napa, Las Vegas, Nevada, and Palladin, Manhattan, New York

SYLVAIN PORTAY: Ritz Carlton, San Francisco, California

THIERRY RAUTUREAU: Rover's, Seattle, Washington

ERIC RIPERT: Le Bernardin, Manhattan, New York

ALESSANDRO STRATTA: Renoir, Las Vegas, Nevada

JEFFREY WEISS: Ritz Carlton, Cleveland, Ohio

Find out more about *Harvesting Excellence*
and the addresses of the producers profiled therein at

www.alain-ducasse.com